D0225636

STRAND PRICE

Czeslaw Milosz and the Insufficiency of Lyric

Czeslaw Milosz

and the Insufficiency of Lyric

BY DONALD DAVIE

THE UNIVERSITY OF TENNESSEE PRESS
KNOXVILLE

Copyright © 1986 by The University of Tennessee Press / Knoxville.
All Rights Reserved. Manufactured in the United States of America.

The paper in this book meets the guidelines for permanence
and durability of the Committee on Production Guidelines
for Book Longevity of the Council on Library Resources.
Binding materials have been chosen for durability.

Library of Congress Cataloging-in-Publication Data

Davie, Donald.
  Czeslaw Milosz and the insufficiency of lyric.

  Bibliography: p.
  Includes index.
  1. Milosz, Czeslaw—Criticism and interpretation.
I. Title. II. Title: Czeslaw Milosz and the
insufficiency of lyric.
PG7158.M5532D38 1985   891.8'58709   85-8028
ISBN 0-87049-483-X

CONTENTS

ACKNOWLEDGMENTS

This book is amplified from the John C. Hodges Lectures delivered at the University of Tennessee in February 1984, under the title "Poetics of the Unfree World: Czeslaw Milosz." I am grateful to the Department of English of the University of Tennessee for an invitation to give the Hodges Lectures, and for much hospitality and amiable consideration extended to my wife and myself in Knoxville.

The substance of "Introduction: *Bells in Winter*" appeared in very different form in *PN Review* 34 and 39 (Manchester, England), and "Appendix: Milosz's War-time Poems" is reprinted almost verbatim from the same journal. I am grateful to Michael Schmidt and *PN Review* for permission to reprint this material.

The author is also grateful to the following for permission to reprint selected excepts:

Farrar, Straus & Giroux, Inc.:
Visions From San Francisco Bay, by Czeslaw Milosz, 1982.

University of California Press:
Emperor of the Earth, Modes of Eccentric Vision, by Czeslaw Milosz, 1977.

Harvard University Press:
The Witness of Poetry, by Czeslaw Milosz, 1983.

The Ecco Press:
Selected Poems, 1980. "No More," "Dedication," "Album of Dreams," "Three Talks on Civilization," "To Robinson Jeffers," "Bobo's Metamorphosis," "The Master," "With Trumpets and Zithers," copyright © 1973 by Czeslaw Milosz.

Bells in Winter, by Czeslaw Milosz, 1978. "Ars Poetica," "Diary of a Naturalist," "The Accuser," copyright © 1978, by Czeslaw Milosz.

The Separate Notebooks, by Czeslaw Milosz, 1984. "The Separate Notebooks: A Mirrored Gallery," "A Book in the Ruins," "The World," "City Without a Name," copyright © 1984 by Czeslaw Milosz.

Donald Davie
Nashville, January 1985

PREFACE
The Issa Valley

For many years anyone of any conscience, reviewing a work by Milosz translated into English, has undertaken in a first paragraph to explain who Czeslaw Milosz is: an explanation that has nearly always resolved itself into, or has taken as its starting point, where Milosz came from. The facts are not in doubt. To follow the best informed of such newspaper reviewers, Neal Ascherson (in the London *Observer,* 26 July 1981), Milosz was born in 1911 "in Lithuania into a family of Polish (or Polonized) gentry." He "witnessed and survived the Nazi onslaught on Poland, the Soviet seizure of Lithuania in 1940, the Nazi Occupation of Poland and the Warsaw Rising of 1945." But already some questions arise. In the first place did the poet witness and survive the rising of 1945 rather than participate in it? (To which the answer seems to be: yes.) And secondly what is hidden behind, or glossed over by, Ascherson's phrase: "Polish (or Polonized)"? Was Milosz's heartfelt response to Lithuania what we are familiar with in the equally heartfelt responses of the Anglo-Irish landowners to Ireland, for instance Elizabeth Bowen's in *Bowen's Court*? And is it therefore, as some Irish critics of Anglo-Irish writing would persuade us, corrupted and discredited at source? Very little in Milosz's most probing investigation of his native Lithuania, his self-styled novel *The Issa Valley* (in Polish 1955, in English 1978), illuminates us about this. He has honorably insisted that the fate of the so-called Baltic republics, Estonia and Latvia as well as Lithuania, is or ought to be a burden on the conscience of the West. But what right has he to speak for Lithuania? And does he assert such a right?

It may not matter. For Milosz, repeatedly though he has dwelt upon his Lithuanian origins (not just in *The Issa Valley*), has consistently offered his witness to the twentieth century as that of a representative and therefore *déraciné* intellectual. To the numerous

English-speakers for whom it is important that the poet in general be distinguished from, if not opposed to, the intellectual, this emphasis in Milosz is unwelcome and must be huddled out of sight so far as possible. One way to do this is to insist on Milosz's "roots" in Lithuania, and this means giving *The Issa Valley* pre-eminence among his works. But the roots were torn up, and although those roots, Polish-cum-Lithuanian in a tangle that no outsider and perhaps few Poles can understand, have indeed been laid bare by Milosz in a way that is absorbing and pathetic, yet the uprooting itself is the postulate that we are invited to proceed from. The argument-from-origins, nowadays seen to be logically untenable in such matters as etymology, is both logically and humanly unacceptable when applied to a life like Milosz's because it would narrow him into being a very special case; and Milosz, who has his own civilly disguised arrogance, has shown that he resents that. Certainly an examination of his origins is illuminating, but one must beware of cramping him back into a context that he, with the help of appalling history, has burst out of.

The Issa Valley, accordingly, is one book by Milosz that needs to be approached with caution. And not all its admirers have been cautious. For the Warton Professor of English Literature at Oxford it is "a masterpiece"; and Professor John Bayley means what he says, for he has declared that it takes a masterpiece like *The Issa Valley* "to reveal the sheer unreality of our modern creative modes and poses."[1] One is reluctant to embark on polemic before the lineaments of Milosz have been sketched in with even the broadest brush. But John Bayley's challenge cannot go unanswered because what he calls "the sheer unreality of our modern creative modes and poses" turns out in his account of the matter to speak most often with an American accent; whereas the author of *The Issa Valley,* having served Stalinist Poland as a diplomat, having then in 1951 defected and spent some years in France, has since 1960 been a resident of the U.S.A. To suggest as Bayley does that Milosz is possessed of an Old World wisdom such as the New World can never learn, seems near to convicting him of ingratitude toward the nation that gave him shelter; and such an impression is at odds with the strenuous attention—critical indeed but also sympathetic—that Milosz for many years has paid to

1. John Bayley, *Selected Essays* (Cambridge, 1984), p. 202.

North American reality, North American society, and North America's cultural traditions.

Moreover, embarrassing though it is to say so, the work that John Bayley esteems so highly is not available to English-speakers in anything like the shape, or with anything like the flavor, that it had when it left the author's hands. Milosz's translators have served him sometimes well, sometimes less well. For many years now he has been very lucky in the translators he has found, particularly for his verse; and he deserves some credit for apparently collaborating with his translators very closely. But the translator of *The Issa Valley* was, though adventurous and enterprising, plainly incompetent. To see this, one need not have the original Polish in hand; simply as an English-speaker knowing only English, one perceives that *The Issa Valley* in English does not hang together. Some reviewers — in truth, depressingly few — recognized that the translator's English wobbled uncertainly between American and British idiom and achieved consistency in neither. He was rather obviously translating word for word, or phrase for phrase, rather than envisaging the actuality that the Polish words registered and then finding the English words, whether American or British, that would convey it. In consequence one personage after another in the narrative, one description after another, one event after another, is rendered in such a way as to defeat the earnest reader's wish to *see*, to envisage. Time and again, for instance, the spatial disposition of people and things is, in the English version of *The Issa Valley*, so unaccountable as to be surreal. And so what John Bayley wants us particularly to esteem in this book, the alleged *solidity* of things and persons and scenes in a lovingly re-created provincial milieu — this may or may not be present in the original, but from the English version that most of us must consult it is conspicuously absent. Contours flow and melt, people behave in unaccountable ways, and in the outcome rural Lithuania between the wars comes to seem a landscape painted by Salvador Dali.

The matter is really of some importance in the case of an author whom we read perforce in translation. Bayley writes: "A poet so good that he can be translated is a supreme paradox, one which many poets of today, and many readers of poetry, would refuse to recognize, so strong is the tendency now for poetry only to congeal and inhere in the carefully exploited accuracies and idiosyncrasies of language." It

is to be hoped that many readers of poetry will warm to this sentiment and think it timely. But that is quite different from asserting
that Czeslaw Milosz is such an infinitely translatable poet, or that
his prose in *The Issa Valley* is a case in point. When Bayley claims
that "In the case of Milosz experience emerges as a quality that over-
rides the impossibilities of translation," what he is saying in fact is
that genius—or, to use his own word, the "experience" of genius—
can override or overcome not just translation but also mistransla-
tion. Mere common sense, but also the dispiriting experience of trying to read *The Issa Valley* in English, reveal that this is not true.
One glimpses—by snatches, and calling on all the generosity one can
muster—what *The Issa Valley* may have been when it emerged from
Milosz's pen or his typewriter, but that certainly is not what one experiences when reading *The Issa Valley* in English translation.

What then led so good a critic as John Bayley to argue a case
so implausible? There is no way to answer that question except by
imputing motives. And, setting aside the all too obvious imputation
of anti-Americanism, one may settle instead, hesitantly, on thinking
that Bayley is too ready to find virtue in rootedness. Although Milosz
ardently partakes of such sentiments for "roots" (as *The Issa Valley*,
with all its imperfections, sufficiently shows), yet he will not endorse
such sentiments as a platform for political action. That much is clear
from his Introduction to a translation of Witkiewicz's *Insatiability*[2]:

> It was only towards the middle of the twentieth century that the in-
> habitants of many European countries came, in general unpleasantly,
> to the realization that their fate could be influenced directly by intri-
> cate and abstruse books of philosophy. Their bread, their work, their
> private lives began to depend on this or that decision in disputes on
> principles to which, until then, they had never paid any attention. . . .
> The average human being, even if he had once been exposed to it, wrote
> philosophy off as utterly impractical and useless. Therefore the great
> intellectual work of the Marxists could easily pass as just one more
> variation on a sterile pastime. Only a few individuals understood the
> causes and probable consequence of this general indifference.

Moreover these words, whether or not they had been written before
The Issa Valley, had certainly been printed before it—originally in

---

2. Stanislaw Ignacy Witkiewicz, *Insatiability*, translated by Louis Iribarne (Illi-
nois 1977, London 1985), p. vii.

The Captive Mind (1953). Whatever Milosz's motive for writing *The Issa Valley*—whether nostalgic indulgence or something more substantial (and from the unsatisfactory English version it is impossible to tell)—he had already seen, before that book was published, that the "things" of a provincial pre-ideological life, however their seeming solidity might years later seem to offer a stay to such as John Bayley, in fact provided no resistance to the honeycombing and undermining activities of a philosophical ideology, once that had penetrated to such communities or had been imposed on them. It was that historically later sort of public life, shot through with ideology, that Milosz in his prose and particularly in his poems would be principally concerned with.

Czeslaw Milosz and the Insufficiency of Lyric

INTRODUCTION
Bells in Winter

This book should be seen as no more than an extended essay. The idea for it, or the possibility of it, was revealed to me only two or three years ago when I gladly fell in with a plan to celebrate one of my British contemporaries whom I most admire: the poet, C.H. Sisson. It seemed to me that the least I could do, to applaud my distinguished compatriot on his seventieth birthday, was measure him up against a contemporary from outside the English-speaking world — a compliment that we English-speakers too seldom pay to our writers. And I had in mind also, as a thoroughly selfish motive, that this would enable me to come to terms with a book I had lately bought: Milosz's *Bells in Winter,* which had left me on a first impatient scanning baffled and even, if the truth be told, more than a little irritated. I knew of Milosz of course, had known of him for more than thirty years, having during that period indulged an amateurish and intermittent interest in Polish poetry generally. But I had not through those decades followed his poetic career, being indeed debarred from doing so, had I wanted to, by the very scant and ill-documented information that was available to us English-speakers who have no Polish. In the event, I found, the English poet Sisson held up his side of the comparison very respectably indeed; but the Polish poet opened before me quite dizzying vistas, as I pressed him into service.

In particular I discovered that Milosz compelled me to re-think the nature of poetic discourse, as distinct from discourse of other kinds. What particularly occasioned this was a poem by my compatriot which I thought, as I think it still, very lovely and affecting. This was "In the West Country" (first published in *PN Review,* 28):

> So it is with Engellond.
> Whose bones rest here? Who was found
> Lying there beside King Arthur's?

Whose bones followed after
Everywhere through the land?
Not a thing one can understand
Name nor yet enumerate.
Yet we are with it and the great
Ancestors lie with the small
Not disturbing us at all
Yet we inhabit with them all
And cannot forget them, or if we do
It is not because they ask us to.
Even Brutus who came from Troy
And landed at Totnes, so they say,
Fought with giants, like that of Cerne
Who held the island in those times.
So it was. That much is firm.

The Sisson who said "That much is firm," of the fabulous history
of Brutus landing at Totnes to found Albion as third Troy, could not
be—I had no difficulty in recognizing—the same C.H. Sisson who
might in an acidulous review in the *Times Literary Supplement* use
the same phrase of some quite different proposition. He expected
us to understand that, and to make whatever allowances were called
for: this assertion, like all the others in the poem, was advanced as
true only within the context and the mood scrupulously established
in the poem's first lines: a day early in the year "within the circle /
Of low hills, I know its ways / Somerton Moor, slight hills, great
girdle / Green floor. . . ."

I had, and have, no difficulty taking the lovely and affecting verses
in this way, making this sort of allowance. But what was borne in
on me, as I measured these English verses against the much spikier
pages of *Bells in Winter,* was that Milosz never gives himself that
sort of latitude, never asks for that sort of allowance.

Not for a moment did I suppose that I had uncovered one of those
chalk-and-cheese distinctions, between language used responsibly (by
Milosz) and irresponsibly (by Sisson). Within the conventions that
govern poetic utterance, still operative in our day though seldom
stated, Sisson's use of language was thoroughly responsible and hon-
est. What I seemed to have discovered in Milosz was a poet who found
no use for one set of such conventions, those that govern the meditative lyric. In such poems—Gray's "Elegy" is one of them surely, and
Wordsworth's "Tintern Abbey" is another—the poet occupies a fixed

point in a landscape, and the assertions that he makes are to be understood as true only in relation to that fixed point, in the context of a special occasion and a mood which that occasion provokes. Sisson's "In the West Country" observed those conventions; no poem in *Bells in Winter* observed them, for the good reason (as I now noticed) that the speaker of those poems occupied no fixed point for the duration of his poem but on the contrary was always flitting, moving about. And that I saw was what had baffled, had almost literally disoriented and therefore irritated me.

My English and my Polish poet had enough in common for them to be comparable. They were both Europeans, and pretty much of an age. But beyond that, both of them were for instance deeply implicated in France and in French culture—something that took on more importance as I penetrated further into both bodies of poetry, Milosz's in particular. In "Diary of a Naturalist," one of the long poems in several sections to be found in *Bells in Winter,* we read for instance:

> What happened there, many would know, I think,
> Who in the parking lot at Roc Amadour
> Found a space and then counted the steps
> To the upper chapel, to make sure that this was it:
> Because a wooden Madonna with a child in a crown
> Was surrounded by a throng of impassive art lovers.
> As I did. Not a step further. Mountains and valleys
> Crossed. Through flames. Wide waters. And unfaithful memory.
> The same passion but I hear no call.
> And the holy had its abode only in denial.

"The same passion but I hear no call. . . ." Here in the originally Roman Catholic Milosz I detected a note that I was familiar with in the originally Anglican Sisson, a note carried indeed (so I could persuade myself) on an identically dry and falling cadence. Neither poet seemed to speak as unequivocally a Christian believer—rather the contrary; but neither could leave alone the central tenets and claims of the Christian Revelation, which instead they continually circled around in a way that seemed designed by both of them to defeat any attempt to affix any one label: "agnostic," "atheist," "lapsed believer."

More surprisingly, both of my poets, in their circlings around Christianity, expressed from time to time something which, though certainly familiar from Christian meditations through the centuries, is rarely met with in our own day: an agonized concern with, and mostly distaste for, their own carnality. In another poem from *Bells in Winter*, "The Accuser," the accusing voice says to the poet:

> Confess, you have hated your body,
> Loving it with unrequited love. It has not fulfilled
> Your high expectations. As if you were chained to
> Some little animal in perpetual unrest.
> Or worse, to a madman, and a Slavic one at that.

A few lines later the physical organs are described as "Sweet and faithful animals"; but the phrase is inside quotation marks, as if to show that this is a view of the human body that the poet knows about, but cannot share. And the accusing voice goes on:

> Do you remember your text book of Church History?
> Even the color of the page, the scent of the corridors.
> Indeed, quite early you were a gnostic, a Marcionite,
> A secret taster of Manichaean poisons.
> From our bright homeland cast down to the earth,
> Prisoners delivered to the ruin of our flesh
> Unto the Archon of Darkness. His is the house and law.
> And this dove, here, over Bouffalowa Street
> Is his as you yourself are. Descend, fire.
> A flash—and the fabric of the world is undone.

Here, in what I register as a passage from Milosz at his most majestic, he surely plunges into blasphemy. For "the dove . . . over Bouffalowa Street," at the same time as it is the Pentecostal dove, the Holy Ghost descending, appears to be also the ultimate nuclear explosion; and the one no less than the other is asserted to be under the Prince of Darkness, whose seat is said to be—as gnostics and Manichaeans believe, but orthodox Christians do not—*the flesh.* (The flesh of course is only the most intimately known item of Nature, which in Manichaean thought is held to be accursed throughout.)

The matter of France re-appears, though seemingly only in a trivial way. For "The Accuser" proceeds with a seductive passage which to an English-speaker can hardly fail to recall T.S. Eliot's "Ash Wednesday" and possibly also some passages of his *Four Quartets*. It begins, "The road weaves upward accompanied by a drum and a flute," and describes a dream-journey by the poet restored to childhood, ending magically in an enchanted castle:

6

Parquetry of dim rooms. Yes, you were expected.
You don't have to say who you are. Everyone here knows and
   loves you.
Eyes meeting eyes, hands touching hands. What communion.
What timeless music of saved generations.

And whoever that man is, from Provence, judging by his dress,
His words, when he addresses beautiful ladies, old men and
   youths,
Are yours as well, as if he and you had long been one:
"Behold the sword that separates Tristan and Iseult.
Revealed to us was the contradiction between life and truth.
In the forgetting of earthly years is our movement and peace.
In our prayer for the last day is our consolation."

Why is the speaker in the dream thought to be "from Provence"? My
guess was that he is provençal because the Provence of the trouba-
dours, at the same time as it invented for the West a very strained
and esoteric cult of AMOR, at the same time, by no means acciden-
tally, fostered the allegedly Manichaean heresies of the Albigensians
and Cathars. I found afterward that this guess was correct, and that
other readers had picked up the clues before me—not surprisingly,
for when I looked into Milosz's prose I found that the trail was heavily marked. Some pages of the autobiography *Native Realm* (1968),
and still more explicitly an essay of the 1960s called "A Short Digres-
sion on Woman as a Representative of Nature," left no doubt that
at this period of his life these were indeed the paths that Milosz was
following; and that, whatever the facts about Catharist beliefs and
practices in old Languedoc—for there are scholars who would reject
the Manichaean slur—Milosz at any rate believed in the connection,
though he indeed might not have thought that imputing Manichaeanism to the Cathars was any sort of slur on them.

   My purpose however is less to expound this poem, "The Accuser,"
richly though it deserves and rewards such exposition, than with a
conspicuous difference that I now became aware of between Milosz
and C.H. Sisson—a difference not in their themes and concerns but
in their poetic procedures. No one who has read even a few of Sisson's poems can fail to recognize that behind them is a philosophical
mind—both in a general sense, and in the sense that this author has
wrestled with philosophical, for instance epistemological, dilemmas.
Yet when I set Milosz beside him, I was forced to recognize that Sis-

son had for many years needed to be sure that he, and also his readers, knew when he was being "philosophical" (in prose) and when "poetic" (in verse). The philosophical dilemmas—for instance, about personal identity—may be recognizably the same in some of Sisson's poems as in some of his prose; but they appear in the verse scrupulously purged of all the jargon of the schools, of any terms like "Platonic," "Hegelian," "Antinomian," "Solipsist." It is quite different with Milosz, who unblushingly carries over from his prose into his verse a technical or semitechnical term like "Manichaean." As between my two poets, it became clear that Milosz had the more voracious, one might almost say the grosser, appetite—not for experience as such, but for its particularities and angularities, the plethora of *names* that we attach to experience in all of its varieties, varieties that we haplessly try to control by sorting them into categories.

It was natural to wonder if this difference between my poets was not related to the one I had noticed first, between the fixed standpoint of the meditative lyrist in Sisson's "Burrington Combe" and the flitting, changeable standpoints of the speakers in Milosz's poems. And I thought I saw the connection: Sisson, I came to see, was interested only in being a lyrist, a *lyrical* poet; whereas Milosz characteristically seeks poetic forms more comprehensive and heterogeneous than any lyric, even the most sustained and elaborate. This is, I should warn the reader, the principal and governing insight that I have come to about Milosz; in the rest of this essay I shall hold by this notion, elaborating on it and pursuing its implications—for an understanding of Milosz but also of poetry more generally.

Undoubtedly Milosz has in his time written lyrics. An important series of short poems from Warsaw and Cracow in the 1940s are certainly lyrics; if they are taken to be something else, they will be misunderstood and can give offense, as we shall see. There is evidence indeed that Milosz in the 1930s began his writing career as a lyrist; in modern times it would be a strange poet who thought to start in any other way. However—and here comes an important point about how we have to proceed—much of Milosz's poetry is not yet available in English, and of that which has been made available the chronology is far from certain. Indeed that chronology has been withheld from us in a way that seems nothing short of perverse. Thus any consideration of his poetry for English-speakers has to be strung on a line of argument, since we lack the materials for a more straightforward and appealing approach: a simple narrative of the poet's career from first to last. This is unfortunate. For Milosz is certainly a poet who has "developed," even over the last twenty or twenty-five years, not to speak of his earlier life. Where I seem to see evidence of this I shall draw attention to it, while acknowledging that the paucity of the chronological record makes such observations hazardous. I shall try not to jump about, more than I have to, from early to late and back again in Milosz's career; but some such high-handedness with the chronological record is unavoidable. The cost of it must be counted.

For the moment, with *Bells in Winter,* we are mostly concerned with the poet at something past the mid-point of his career, in the first decade of his permanent residence in the U.S.A., specifically in California. And since, as I have explained, I chanced to engage with *Bells in Winter* in a specifically British context (one, it must be said, that Milosz has never shown much if any interest in), it is worth staying with that context a little longer. The reviews of *Bells in Winter* in the British press reveal by and large a reluctant shaking of heads. Damning with faint praise is what the British mostly came up with. "In the end, a tantalizing collection," wrote Mark Abley in *The Literary Review.* But for this, he hastened to add, not author or translator or publisher was to blame. Rather the trouble was, precisely, Milosz's indifference to lyrical purity: "Packed with references to history, natural history and theology, they are poems with a breadth of civilization at their command, and unless we share something of Milosz's learning much of their effect is diluted." But this of course is just what worried and diffident readers have said over two generations about Eliot and Pound, Charles Olson and Basil Bunting—an important point, since it reminds us that, if C.H. Sisson mostly chooses to stay within the conventions of the lyrical standpoint, there were English-language poets before him who had not. As if uneasily aware of this, Mark Abley (who deserves respect—I am not jeering at him) shifted his ground; no, on second thoughts, "the central difficulty . . . is linguistic"—how much, we must think, has been lost in translation. Julian Symons in *The Sunday Times,* a more practised reviewer, was too old a hand to get trapped into sounding like a bewildered early reader of Eliot's *The Waste Land.* Instead he shook his head along with the much-lost-in-translation school: "How much of a poet's qualities are seen in translation is always doubtful . . . Milosz comes through pretty well. . . ." ("Pretty well"—surely the dustiest bouquet of 1981.) Julian Symons told his readers that in *Bells in Winter* "the prevailing tone is chatty, comic and wayward, lightly brushed with surrealism"; whereas, if those readers subscribed also to another magazine, *Critical Quarterly,* they would have learned bewilderingly from the reviewer there, Alan Young, that Milosz "rarely relaxes into the frivolous or even the lightweight." The point is surely that both Symons and Young are right: as the standpoint of the speaker changes, so does the tone that he addresses us in—abandoning the fixed standpoint of the lyrically meditative "I," Milosz necessarily offends also against the decorous requirement that the speaker maintain a consistent tone.

Particularly interesting was a piece in *Poetry Review* by D.M. Thomas, who was in 1981 still short of the international celebrity that was to come to him as a best-selling scandalous novelist. Thomas, though he dutifully acknowledged "the limitations of translation," could not push far along that line because he was reviewing *Bells in Winter* along with two other collections in translation, Joseph Brodsky's *A Part of Speech* and Andrei Voznesensky's *Nostalgia for the Present,* both of which he wanted to praise; and so it was Thomas, himself an accomplished verse-translator from the Russian, who came right out and said what Abley and Symons and other reviewers implied: "I found *Bells in Winter* disappointing." For Thomas, as between Brodsky and Milosz there was no comparison, even though the Russian poet has called the Pole "one of the greatest poets of our time, perhaps the greatest." Grounds for comparison existed, however, between Milosz and the other Russian, Voznesensky. Voznesensky is, so Thomas assures us, a vulgarian; but all the same he has "leaping imagination and zestfulness" which "puts our insular poets to shame." He is moreover "warm, humane, direct," whereas in *Bells in Winter* "the poems are abstract, unpeopled. There is little human warmth."

In fact, the poems of *Bells in Winter* are abundantly peopled. It is there that we encounter for instance, in "Diary of a Naturalist," "Spleeny Baginski in checkered knickers." But one takes D.M.

Thomas's point: Baginski may be named in a warm tone, but his knickers hardly can be. If checkered knickers and similarly obdurate facts (for instance of theology—Marcionites, Manichaeans) are to be named in poetry, the tone of that poetry must be something less than heated. Accordingly, not just D.M. Thomas and Julian Symons but many readers will register Milosz's tone in his poems as aggravatingly *cool.* He has his ardors, his fevers even, as we shall see; but the warmth is very seldom that of the lyrical poet uttering his private torments and exaltations directly to whatever sympathetic reader is capable of responding to them with equal ardor. In particular, Thomas's review enables us to nail one persistent misunderstanding: Milosz is at all points very far from that "nightingale fever" which characterizes his great Russian precursors—Mandelstam and Tsvetayeva, Akhmatova and Pasternak. Any attempt to treat him as an associate of theirs (all Slavs together, as it were) is sure to find him, as Donald Thomas did, disappointing. This difference between Milosz and the Russians is immediately apparent from his poems; it is discernible particularly in the tone of voice with which his poems address us from the page—a tone that is often tauntingly sober and disenchanted, as his Russian peers seldom are. But it is backed up, as we might expect, by a difference that is philosophical or ideological. In a way that we have prepared ourselves for, Milosz asserts: "My contemporaries (strongly affected by Manichaeanism, and like it or not, I am one of them) have moved far from any doctrines espousing harmony with nature and the wise acceptance of its rhythms as a guide to behavior. . . ." And elsewhere in *Visions from San Francisco Bay* he declares:

> If I regarded nature sentimentally, I would treat virtue with less respect. Since nature is not a loving mother but ravages and kills us without qualms if we find ourselves in it without weapons or tools, virtue must be held in high esteem, for it alone permits the effective use of weapons and tools. The courage (*fortitudo*) of which Cicero speaks may reside in the evil and the good, the wise and the foolish. It manifests itself in situations that exist independent of our will, and it commands us to behave in one definite way and no other.

This alleged virtue, since it may reside equally "in the evil and the good," should probably be translated by the Italian term *virtù,* for which modern Anglo-American supplies no equivalent. At any rate we find here, though without any touch of technocratic enthusiasm, Milosz's approval of technology ("weapons and tools"), and his prayer for the virtue, *fortitudo,* that knows how to handle technology. Elsewhere, refugee though he is from state-imposed Marxism, Milosz recognizes how Marxism derives from this persuasion that he shares, of how Nature is "a callous mother":

> The liberation of man from subjection to the market is nothing but his liberation from the power of nature, because the market is an extension of the struggle for existence and nature's cruelty, in modern society. . . . Marxism is thus in harmony with the neo-Manichaean ferocity of modern man. Were it not, it would not exercise the near-magical attraction it has for the most active minds and would not be a central concern for philosophers.

None of the modern masters in poetry share this Darwinian conviction that Nature is a callous mother; or else, if they do share it, none of them cares to articulate it with anything like Milosz's sober insistence. Certainly the Russian masters do not; all of them — even Mandelstam, whom Milosz particularly venerates — are nature-poets, such as Milosz in all honesty could not be.

Not just in the Slavic cultures but world-wide this challenge that Milosz throws down has to be met. Donald Carne-Ross for instance, no Slavist and equally no Little-Englander but a haughty Hellenist, has declared (in *Instaurations,* 1979): "And yet poetry is naturally, in the old sense, pagan, and poets are the great autochthons. They are in love with earth and its seasonal rhythms, its recurring transience." It may be that Carne-Ross is right; most of us act as if we think he is. But in that case the Milosz of the 1960s can hardly be a poet at all. What has to be noted in any case is that Carne-Ross's burying or dispersal of the divine in the natural — something he finds everywhere in archaic Greece, and then intermittently though splendidly recovered by a modern master like Pound — depends on an acceptance, explicit in Carne-Ross, implicit and indeed unconscious in others, of Nietzsche's saying: "God" (meaning the Christian God) "is dead." Believer or not, Milosz will not accept that. So far from the cruelty of Nature making against the Christian's God, it is only belief in God that makes the cruelty of Nature acceptable and understandable, since He belongs in, and so proves the reality of, a *supernatural* realm, which may be called Grace. At any rate, issues as far-reaching as this are involved (so I suggest) in what may seem at first sight only a pedantic dispute about nomenclature: the question whether a body of poetry may or may not be described as "lyrical."

Milosz's most considered response to his Russian peers is an essay of 1963, "On Pasternak Soberly," together with a piece written six years later which immediately follows the Pasternak essay in *Emperor of the Earth. Modes of Eccentric Vision* (1977); this latter a vehemently and appealingly unguarded declaration, "On Modern Russian Literature and the West," quite plainly from the pen of an indignantly concerned poet rather than a professor of Slavic literatures. On the essay about Pasternak I may at last speak with a certain authority, having myself devoted many years not as scholar but as poet to an admiring and entranced study of Pasternak's poetry. And I do not hesitate to declare that Milosz's few pages press to the heart of the challenge that Pasternak's literary witness throws down to us, in a way that no other document known to me can equal.

As Milosz sees the matter, Pasternak's challenge has everything to do with the status of lyrical discourse, and with the special privileges that the lyrical poet demands, and is commonly, even in the Soviet Union, accorded. Seeing Pasternak through the lens of analogous Polish lyrists of his time, notably Julian Tuwim, Milosz protests:

> They seemed to elude the dilemma which for my generation was insoluble but oppressive: for us a lyrical stream, a poetic idiom liberated from the chores of discourse, was not enough, the poet should also be a *thinking* creature; yet in our efforts to build a poem as an "act of mind" we encountered an obstacle: speculative thought is vile, cunning, it eats up the internal resources of a poet from inside.

The enduring value of Milosz's testimony about Pasternak resides precisely in the fact that the dilemma here honestly confessed is nowhere in Milosz's essay solved or transcended. Pasternak's intransigently and uncompromisingly lyrical witness —"Pasternak's poetry is antispeculative, anti-intellectual. It is poetry of sensory perception" —did in fact, as a matter of historical record in the ugly *brouhaha* attending the award to him of the Nobel Prize in 1968, challenge the technocratic and bureaucratic assumptions of the modern state (whether totalitarian or not) as no other poetic witness has done; and yet, for that challenge to be thrown down in a way that could not be ignored, Pasternak had to diverge from his chosen vocation as lyrical poet so far as to write the novel, *Doctor Zhivago*. Thus Milosz's attitude to Pasternak remains profoundly ambiguous:

> . . . I tend to accuse Pasternak . . . of a programmatic helplessness in the face of the world, of a carefully cultivated irrational attitude. Yet it was exactly this attitude that saved Pasternak's art and perhaps his life in the sad Stalinist era. Pasternak's more intellectually inclined colleagues answered argument by argument, and in consequence they were either liquidated or they accepted the supreme wisdom of the official doctrine. Pasternak eluded all categories; the "meaning" of his poems was that of lizards or butterflies, and who could pin down such phenomena using Hegelian terms? He did not pluck fruits from the tree of reason, the tree of life was enough for him. Confronted by argument, he replied with his sacred dance.
>
> We can agree that in the given conditions that was the only victory possible. Yet if we assume that those periods when poetry is amputated, forbidden thought, reduced to imagery and musicality, are not the most healthy, then Pasternak's was a Pyrrhic victory.

After noting, quite correctly I think, that *Doctor Zhivago* is in no sense an anti-Marxist work but on the contrary Marxist ("He seemed to be interpreting Marxism in a religious way"), and after noting with marked distaste Pasternak's liking for the French Jesuit Teilhard de Chardin, Milosz is forced to concede:

> But Pasternak's weaknesses are dialectically bound up with his great discovery. He conceded so much to his adversary, speculative thought, that what remained was to make a jump into a completely different dimension . . . whoever engages in a polemic with the thought embodied in the state will destroy himself for he will become a hollow man. It is impossible to talk to the new Caesar, for then you choose the encounter on his ground. What is needed is a new beginning, new in the present conditions but not new in Russia marked as it is by centuries of Christianity. The literature of Socialist Realism should be shelved and forgotten; the new dimension is that of every man's mysterious destiny, of compassion and faith. In this Pasternak revived the best tradition of Russian literature, and he will have successors. He already has one in Solzhenitsyn.

Thus Pasternak remains for Milosz, as he honestly admits, a paradox. His witness is courageous and admirable, yet he achieved it by means that should not have worked though in the event they did—*lyrical* means. What is clear by the end of Milosz's essay is that he is temperamentally averse to Pasternak's natural bent—what he calls, in a memorable and not unjust phrase, Pasternak's "reedlike pliability." It comes as no surprise that he should in the event declare himself rather for Mandelstam—"for me the ideal of a modern classical poet . . . crystalline, resistant, and therefore fragile." But it was not Mandelstam who survived, but Pasternak—and not at the cost of making any shameful concessions or compromises. Milosz is aware of that, and it disconcerts him.

And in any case, though Milosz chooses not to go into the matter, Mandelstam in his brittle and crystalline way is as much a lyrical poet as Pasternak is. The Russian poet of their generation who rejected the lyrical stance was Vladimir Mayakovsky. And in the essay on Pasternak, Milosz acknowledges him: "Mayakovsky wanted to smash to pieces the image of the poet as a man who withdraws. He wanted to be a Walt Whitman—as the Europeans imagined Walt Whitman." Milosz sympathizes; as we see from his bitter reflection: "Already some hundred years ago poetry had been assigned a kind of reservation for a perishing tribe; having conditioned reflexes we, of course, admire 'pure lyricism.'" But for Milosz, Mayakovsky was a god who failed. The evidence for this is in a poem, the first of "Three Talks on Civilization." Here we read, in a translation by Milosz himself:

> if people (instead of everyday necessity and the, so to speak,
> hairy pleasures proper to the flesh)
> spick-and-span, pretending they do not stink at all,
>
> nibbled chocolates in a theater,
> if they were moved by the loves of Amyntas,
> and in the day time read the *Summa,* luckily too difficult,
>
> none would be fit for the barracks. The State would fall.

These lines have so much authority in English that it is difficult to credit they were originally composed in another tongue. A gloss on them is not hard to find. It is a passage from Milosz's autobiography, *Native Realm,* about Mayakovsky. There we are told: "One syllogism from Thomas Aquinas annihilated him. Whether or not one accepted or rejected that syllogism did not matter; a mind trained on it could not help but be suspicious of words used as an unshackled vital force." Somewhere here, I guess, is the seed of a concern that would occupy Milosz through his American years: a distinction between Walt Whitman as in his American identity he truly is, and what Europeans have made of him. As for Mayakovsky himself, if *Native Realm* did not supply evidence of what a powerful enchanter Mayakovsky was for the young Milosz, there is plenty of other evidence of what an authoritative presence that Russian poet was between the wars in Poland and even (some of us can just remember) in Britain. If we are right to see in Milosz one who sets his face against lyrical "purity" for poets—forced, it may be reluctantly, to that position— we can see how necessary it was for him to distinguish the poet's proper didacticism, which he avowed and espoused and tried to practice, from the vociferously intoxicating "publicism" of a Mayakovsky —to which we might attach, without much injustice, the epithet, "propagandist." Between the private lyricism of a Pasternak (to which he had objections beyond those we have so far considered), and a Mayakovsky's embracing of speculative thought (which is "vile, cunning . . . eats up the internal resources of a poet from inside"), the young Milosz was caught in a bind which it would take him many years to work out of.

As for younger Russians like Andrei Voznesensky, it is entertaining to see Milosz and his correspondent, Aleksandr Wat, agreeing that Voznesensky is "a strip-tease artist"; professing a certain esteem for such performers; yet agreeing that such artists—whether British or Polish, American or Russian—somehow are wide of the mark, concerning the issues that really split apart twentieth-century poetics.

An American reader might well wonder what he has to do with an author like Milosz who naturally locates and defines himself among European influences, European currents and cross-currents—Polish certainly, but also Russian, also French. Does the American reader have any access to such a writer, or any responsibility toward him? Yet the answer is surely clear. In the first place Milosz's exile is now of very long standing; he has been living and writing in the U.S.A. for almost a quarter-century. And in the second place he has been at great pains to earn his passage, to acknowledge that his domestication in the States imposes certain duties on him—that he must, and will, come halfway to meet his American neighbors. Not only do his poems incorporate more and more of American experience and American scenes, but he has also, with the cooperation of an unusually devoted and expert group of collaborators, made over more and more of his Polish poems into English. We might almost say that he has strenuously done his best to turn himself into an American poet—almost we might say that, and yet we cannot because it would imply that Milosz has been prepared to jettison that Polish/Lithuanian part of himself which is ultimately unassimilable. By refusing to take that step Milosz, as he well knows, is refusing the bargain that could not be refused by his less privileged compatriots who flocked off the immigrant ships in the last century to constitute "Polacks," American citizens of Polish ancestry. Milosz's negotiation between the demands of American hospitality and the ungainsayable demands of Lithuanian or of Polish ancestry represents an act of contrition and compassion toward those Polish immigrants who could not become American except at the price of ceasing to be Polish; it was a negotiation possible to him, though painful, partly because when he made the break he had already achieved a measure of international fame, but also because he had already gone through a similar exercise in order to make his Lithuanian identity Polish. (This early transformation would merit an essay all to itself were it not that Milosz himself has given an absorbing account of it in *Native Realm.*) Thus I propose in all humility, as myself a resident alien in the U.S., that Milosz's writings represent an unusually compelling record of what is involved for a European in making himself American, or "Americanized." In this way his claim on American readers' attention is a *human* claim—a plea to be understood with sympathy, as in some degree a representative case.

On the other hand Milosz has several times asserted, and more often implied, that his experience under totalitarian regimes, before he defected to the West, has furnished him with certain insights, about the relations between poetry and society, such as we in the West cannot afford to ignore. When I lectured on him I tried to acknowledge this by subtitling my lecture: "Poetics of the Unfree World." I was not unaware that this might be said with an ironic inflection; and I do not resent such irony. We in the parliamentary democracies of the West are, if we are poets and even if we are not, less free than we like to think or than our political leaders would persuade us; and our peers in eastern Europe are free of certain pressures that inhibit us, from commercialized mass-entertainment, for instance. "Free" and "unfree," as I take over the terms from the vocabulary of official hand-outs, must therefore be understood with certain reservations. Even so there is a massively obvious sense in which the United States or the United Kingdom is a free society as communist Poland is not; and it is right to ask, as Milosz wants us to, whether the poetic voca-tion as we in our freedom conceive of it and practice it is not a luxury product. If it is, then it can quite properly be spurned and disowned by the poets of Poland, however far such poets may be from embrac-ing the official ideology of the Polish state. Has not literature, in the democratic West, become politically irresponsible? This is the ques-tion that Milosz puts to us, time and again—never more furiously than in his 1971 essay "On Modern Russian Literature and the West":

> Let me note a formidable paradox: in the countries where Christian churches thrive there are practically no genuinely Christian novels. Truly Christian writing has had to come from Russia, where Christians have been persecuted for several decades. Then how can a critic, if he is a hot-blooded creature and not a frog, placidly bypass such a chal-lenge and not shout on the rooftops his protest against the use made of freedom by Western literati?

It is a question that we cannot afford not to answer. And so this is another reason why the American reader cannot ignore Milosz: he throws down a challenge that has to be met if we, poets and readers of poetry, are to sleep with a good conscience.

On the other hand, erudite though Milosz is and in particular knowledgeable about the strategies and swervings in the present cen-tury of the international *avant-garde,* he is sceptical, sometimes im-patiently, of the pretensions of many intellectuals. On one of the two occasions when I have been with him, we found common ground for conversation in the person of the forgotten Ulsterman Captain Thomas Mayne Reid, hero (somewhat dubiously) of the American assault on Fort Chapultepec in 1847, whose adventure-stories were read by schoolboys in Chekhov's Russia and Milosz's Lithuania as well as by me in Yorkshire, England, in the 1930s. Years later I found an affectionate and informative and serious essay on Mayne in Mi-losz's book, *Emperor of the Earth.* And this gives in one way the measure of the man. He is as likely to concern himself with unfash-ionable books as with fashionable ones. Though in his poems Milosz uses boldly stratagems that we are likely to think of as "modernist," his modernism is in no way programmatic; and indeed for some aspects of international literary modernism he feels nothing but contempt and dislike. In particular he does not suppose that a writer, merely by styling himself "poet," enjoys a superior status to a writer of adventure-stories for schoolboys, or has a right to special privileges denied to writers of a supposedly humbler sort. We need not look to Milosz for ringing declarations about the exalted condition of the poet as seer, visionary, prophet; he would like that to be true (he would very much like it to be true), but he knows it is not. On the contrary he thinks that the writing of poetry is morally and politically a very dubious occupation, and one that continually requires to be justified, never altogether conclusively. In this way he has a lot of sympathy with a reader who is distrustful of literary pretensions.

Similarly, in prose and verse alike, Milosz often seems content with forms that are unpretentious, capacious, that hang together only loosely. A reader would not go far wrong who thought of the longer poems in *Bells in Winter,* to begin with, as so many essays in verse. An essayist — a certain air of genteel fustiness hangs around the word; and this is not inappropriate to a writer who entitles a poem, "Diary of a Naturalist," and incorporates in it prosey entry-headings: "I give a brief account of what happened to a book which was once our favorite. . . ." Moreover this, it seems, is deliberate. For Milosz has written:

> I have always aspired to a more spacious form
> that would be free from the claims of poetry or prose
> and would let us understand each other without exposing
> the author or reader to sublime agonies.

Readers of William Carlos Williams, or of any one of his dozens of imitators, are familiar with poetry cut down to size in this way, and also with large chunks of prose coming in what are offered as poems. What is more arresting is that Milosz finds prose also too constricting. For what can be more "spacious" than prose? Or what claims does prose have on us, that we should want to be free of them? Yet if we think of some names dear to the modernist *avant-garde* — Vladimir Nabokov and Samuel Beckett, Jorge Luis Borges and Boris Pasternak — we recognize that much modern or modernist prose is indeed highly patterned, ornate, to just that degree constricting. And Milosz wants no part of it. What stands to reason, once we think about it, is that when he wants to free himself from such constrictions he does so not by breaking a barrier that confronts him but on the contrary by harking back—to that faded and unfashionable form, the essay. This is experimental writing, sure enough—for what does "essay" mean, if not experiment?—but it is not experimental in a way to fit our technicolored assumption that the experimenter works always at or beyond the frontiers. What is likely to disconcert us most, if we engage with Milosz after an immersion in the international avant-garde, is his unflurried or blithely unconcerned frequenting of authors and kinds of writing that are very much out of fashion. (The same is true, of course, of Borges.)

This should be kept in mind when we approach what must surely be Milosz's most strenuous attempt to explain himself to American readers: his Charles Eliot Norton lectures of 1981–82, published under the title, *The Witness of Poetry*. On the evidence of this slim volume Milosz when he lectures is still an essayist. Each of these six lectures is best regarded as a spoken essay, each an independent rumination. This is not quite true, for the lectures are interconnected; but the connections between them are left loose, certainly they are not interlinked like the stages in an argument. And although I shall have to speak of the book as if it pursued an argument, this is misleading. What I shall try to chart is not a line of argument but rather a drift from first to last; and I shall isolate only one such "drift" among others that might be discerned.

Surprisingly these Harvard lectures, loose-jointed and rambling as they are, have the effect—which Milosz himself may not be wholly aware of, and might not willingly acknowledge—of establishing that, when all is said and done, the World War II experience of eastern Europe, not excluding the appalling experience of East European Jewry, does *not* compel us to conceive of the office of poetry in some unprecedented, disillusioned, and peculiarly exacting way. There have not been lacking voices— some of them sensational, hysterical and even spiteful, others (like Milosz's own voice) genuinely troubled by shame and anger—which have maintained that the explosion of evil under Nazism, in the centre of what had been conceived of as Western European civilization, does indeed compel us to a radical re-thinking of what we had taken for granted as the "office" (the social and/or religious justification) of poetry and of the arts in general. An instance is the perhaps apocryphal but in any case emblematic anecdote of the extermination-camp commandant listening devotedly in his off-duty hours to Brahms; and the conclusion drawn from that by some commentators, that the case reveals the ineffectiveness in the event of Brahms and of the entire Western culture that, for the sake of the argument, Brahms may be thought to represent. Milosz certainly would agree that an experience such as he lived through in Warsaw in the 1940s does exact of us a radical, even corrosive re-thinking of what we are doing when we create art or respond to it. And he has applied himself through 40 years to just such a re-appraisal. Yet the end of his re-thinking, his re-appraisal, is a re-assertion and vindication of the artist's office as traditionally conceived, "classical" as Milosz uses that term—that is to say, as mediated to us from the world of the ancients through the Renaissance.

To perceive this is not in the least to ask Milosz to unsay any of the vehemently wounding allegations of heartless frivolity that he has

justly leveled against the poetry and the poetics of the "free" world
since 1945 — especially against those realms of the free world that
are centered upon, or take their lead from, Paris. The last thing Milosz wants to do is to nourish complacency in the free world, when
it compares itself with the unfree. It is nonetheless true that by the
end of the Harvard lectures Milosz has argued himself into a position that is, as regards poetics, strikingly conservative.

The crucial turn-around and recognition can be located in the
fourth of the lectures, called "A Quarrel with Classicism," where Milosz fascinatingly draws out the implications of one of his own poems.
It is entitled "No More," and we can ponder it in the translation by
Anthony Milosz:

> I should relate sometime how I changed
> My views on poetry, and how it came to be
> That I consider myself today one of the many
> Merchants and artisans of Old Japan,
> Who arranged verses about cherry blossoms,
> Chrysanthemums and the full moon.
>
> If only I could describe the courtesans of Venice
> As in a loggia they teased a peacock with a twig,
> And out of brocade, the pearls of their belt,
> Set free heavy breasts and the reddish weal
> Where the buttoned dress marked the belly,
> As vividly as seen by the skipper of galleons
> Who landed that morning with a cargo of gold;
> And if I could find for their miserable bones
> In a graveyard whose gates are licked by greasy water
> A word more enduring than their last-used comb
> That in the rot under tombstones, alone, awaits the light,
>
> Then I wouldn't doubt. Out of reluctant matter
> What can be gathered? Nothing, beauty at best.
> And so, cherry blossoms must suffice for us
> And chrysanthemums and the full moon.

The first ply of irony, in what is a very ironical poem, can hardly
be missed. "If only I could," he says, "do . . ." what he then proceeds
to do! For how could the Venetian courtesans be re-created more vividly than in the two images he finds for them — the reddish weal left
on the belly, and the last-used comb left intact in the grave-mold when
all else has decomposed? "If only," then, cannot be trusted; it is not

after all any inability on his part to make the vanished past present, that makes him demote himself from the rank of artist to that of skilled (Japanese) artisan. What, then, impels him to this self-demotion? It is dissatisfaction with what such presentative skills leave us with — "beauty at best." An ability equal to say Ezra Pound's, in thus presenting (making present) what is dead and gone, amounts, so Milosz seems to say, to nothing more than the skill of arranging and re-arranging, in a highly conventional art, certain conventional properties — cherry blossoms, chrysanthemums, the moon.

Milosz himself remarks:

> It would seem that the description of Venetian courtesans provides a valid proof of language's capacity to encounter the world. But immediately the speaker undermines that conclusion. This he does most obviously by referring to a painting by Carpaccio, which depicts a yard in Venice where the courtesans are sitting and teasing a peacock with a twig. Thus . . . reality appears as mediated by a work of painting — in other words, not in its original state but already well ordered, already a part of culture. If reality exists, then how are we to dream of reaching it without intermediaries of one or another sort, whether they are other literary works or visions provided by the whole past of art? Thus the protest against conventions, instead of taking us to some free space where a poet can encounter the world directly, as on the first day of Creation, again sends us back to those historical strata that already exist as form.

The argument is irrefutable, and is proved every hour of the working day of any responsible artist in any medium: art *is* artifice, all art operates within a frame of conventions, including for instance those different sets of conventions which distinguish one poetic *genre* from another. Though so obvious to the producers of art, this fact is often not obvious at all to the consumers, the artists' publics; and of course there are always dishonest or stupid artists who are at pains to delude the public into thinking that *they* at any rate have escaped the webs of convention so as to "encounter the world directly." And yet, though the argument is irrefutable, it is also, for Milosz, unacceptable. Here comes the second ply of irony, for whereas the poem says, "cherry blossoms must suffice," it is plain that for the writer of the poem they do *not* suffice. He cannot refute his own argument, and yet he rebels at it. In case the bitter irony in the last lines is not apparent from the poem itself, let us hear the poet, speaking I think with moving eloquence. The description of Venetian courtesans, says Milosz, "paradoxically shows us the poet achieving what, in his opinion, was beyond his power." But, Milosz goes on,

> Since this entire image is in the conditional and has to serve as a proof of the insufficiency of words, it is not a description which would satisfy the poet and is at best an outline, a project. Beyond the words used, a presence is felt, of entire human lives condensed: these courtesans at the moment they receive a skipper of galleons, their fate, imaginable but not told, their death, their last-used comb. The real is simply too abundant; it wants to be named, but names cannot embrace it and it remains no more than a catalogue of data devoid of any ultimate meaning.

This artist, we see, is unappeasable. He wants his art to do what of its very nature (as he knows very well) it cannot do: register, name "the real" in all its abundance.

It is very important to distinguish Milosz's complaint about "the insufficiency of words" from certain more far-reaching complaints about language which have exercised philosophers and poets for at least 300 years, most notably though of course not exclusively in France. This more thorough-going disenchantment with language, inaugurated perhaps by Descartes, asks what proof we have that our words, *any* of our words, name a reality outside of ourselves. How do we prove that language does more than name our perceptions, that is to say a reality internal to ourselves, inside our own heads or hearts; our wishes, sentiments, misapprehensions and misconstructions, yearnings and hungers? How can we be sure that "the real," conceived of as something other than us and unsmirched by us and our needs, is at all accessible to us, or at any rate to our language? Indeed, if we cannot prove this, how can we know that "the real," as thus conceived of, exists outside our perhaps deluded notions of it? This debate continues, and no doubt it is interminable. Milosz however has no patience with it. For him the existence of the real, the Other, the "out there," is a *datum,* a given, something that he refuses to argue about, at whatever risk of being thought philosophically naive. His complaint is not (with Descartes) that language has no demonstrable access to such a "real," but that it has access to all too little of it. For Milosz, language in the hands of a poet does indeed have access to the real, but not to the real in all its abundance.

It names right enough, it names reliably and accurately, but it names too little. When pushed to the wall, and sometimes when not so pushed, Milosz will imply angrily that such nice epistemological dilemmas, however insoluble in their own terms, reveal themselves as frivolous when mankind is *in extremis,* as in Warsaw in the 1940s.

Milosz also teases out of the poem, "No More," an implication which, without his guidance, we might well have missed. Although in the poem as a whole the speaker's wish to identify himself with "Merchants and artists of Old Japan" is, as we have seen, not to be taken at face value, nevertheless when the phrase first occurs in the fourth line it does represent a social status that he yearns for. As he explains:

> "Merchants and artisans of Old Japan," average people who practised poetry in their free moments, are introduced in order to stress the integral place of the versifier's craft in the habits of all society. We have here a radical renouncement of the heritage of bohemia, with its pride in the isolated and alienated poet.

The context makes it clear that when Milosz wrote "the habits of all society," what he meant was something like "the habits of all societies before, and except, our own." For when Milosz, characteristically much happier with the socio-historical than with the philosophical dimensions of his topic, expatiates on the versifier's role and status in society, he begins to tell us things that we are perhaps wearily familiar with. There has been no lack of English-language poets telling us, over the years, how the conspicuously marginal status of the poet in our societies is an aberration and an abnormality; how, in all societies that we have record of including the most primitive, the office of poet has been given honor and esteem and centrality such as our societies are quite plainly withholding from it.

On this matter Milosz seems to have little more to say than we have heard from others, or can enunciate for ourselves. With him, as with those others, we find ourselves in no time at all faced with the well-known quandary about the chicken and the egg. Briefly, did Stéphane Mallarmé and the modernists following him go out of their way to affront what might have been their audience? Or did that potential audience, the "beastly bourgeois," so plainly reveal his intolerance that the responsible artist was left no dignified recourse but to affront him? For Milosz, as for other speakers on this burning topic, the names crucially in question are French: Flaubert and Mallarmé. And at least on Flaubert I take it he is simply wrong:

> . . . was Flaubert contradicting the bourgeoisie or contradicting life? This is not clear because for Flaubert ordinary people epitomized life in general, which was as dreary as the existence of woodlice. The separation of art and the public has been an accomplished fact ever since.

I do not recognize in this description the author of "Un Coeur Simple," nor of that comic and compassionate masterpiece, *Bouvard et Pécuchet.* Accordingly, I find more reasons than Milosz does for thinking that the fastidious retreat of a Mallarmé into the haughtily alienated Bohemia, *l'art pour l'art,* was forced upon him by insupportable behavior on the part of society, of a society that was prepared to prosecute Baudelaire for *Les Fleurs du Mal,* and Flaubert for *Madame Bovary.*

These are old quarrels which there is little point in inflaming afresh. If a *bourgeoisie* still exists, at least in the English-speaking nations, it is surely characterized by an amoral permissiveness and calloused levity rather than by any disposition to prosecute artists for telling unpalatable truths. Indeed, the more unpalatable the truth, the more likely it is to re-activate the jaded palate of today's tired business person. And so it is hard not to think that when Milosz retells these old stories to illuminate the present situation of the serious artist in the free world, he is tilting at figures of straw. Nor is he persuasive when, on this issue, he would have us believe that his Polish experience and his Polish inheritance have furnished him with specially valuable insights. After all, if Milosz wants the secure status and esteem of the (perhaps legendary) Japanese artisan, then he must accept the constraints which such an artisan or artificer is inured to in traditional societies. And it is rather plain that Milosz is not ready to accept such constraints: on the contrary, as confessedly an heir of the Polish Romantics, he dreams (vainly, as he knows) of being accepted as prophet and seer, practicing a sort of poetry that he has called "eschatological," "millennial," or (the slogan of his youth in the '30s) "catastrophist." Milosz disarms us by frankly confessing that on this issue he is not just in two minds but is contradicting himself: "My aim here has been to indicate a contradiction that resides at the very foundation of the poet's endeavor." And yet the truth seems to be that we have here touched on a sore spot in Milosz's thinking; one that, early and late, he cannot forbear rubbing at and inflaming. Though there is no reason to think he has ever regretted his defection to the "free" world, grievously though he has paid for it, he retains from his communist or populist youth a conviction that there must be a social role for the poet beyond that which he calls "bohemian"; and he never ceases to accuse and scorn those poets of the "free" world who have accepted the bohemian role. Once again it is the 1963 essay on Pasternak which confronts the issue most directly:

> Like many of his contemporaries in various countries, he drew upon the heritage of French *poètes maudits*. In every avant-garde movement, the native traditions expressed through the exploration of linguistic possibilities are perhaps more important than any foreign influences. I am not concerned, however, with literary genealogy but with an image which determines the poet's tactics—an image of himself and of his rôle. A peculiar image was created by French poets of the nineteenth century, not without help from the minor German romantics and Edgar Allan Poe; this image soon became common property of the international avant-garde. The poet saw himself as a man estranged from a society serving false values, an inhabitant of *la cité infernale,* or, if you prefer, of the wasteland, and passionately opposed to it. He was the only man in quest of true values, aware of surrounding falsity, and had to suffer because of his awareness. Whether he chose rebellion or contemplative art for art's sake, his revolutionary technique of writing served a double purpose: to destroy the automatism of opinions and beliefs transmitted through a frozen, inherited style; and to mark his distance from the idiom of those who lived false lives. Speculative thought, monopolized by optimistic philistines, was proclaimed taboo: the poet moved in another realm, nearer to the heart of things. Theories of two languages were elaborated: *le langage lyrique* was presented as autonomous, not translatable into any logical terms proper to *le langage scientifique.*

Milosz, as we have seen and shall see again, constantly refuses this distinction: in his poems he stubbornly uses *le langage scientifique* along with *le langage lyrique,* in such a way as to imply that they belong together in one common universe of discourse. He has no patience with what has been called the "Two Truths" theory of knowledge, according to which scientific language does not have to be reconciled with lyrical language since each is true "in its own terms," in terms of the universe of discourse which each inhabits and appeals to, two universes which are held to be not in competition since at no point do they touch or overlap. By refusing to sign this amiable treaty of non-intervention, Milosz sets himself at odds with most Anglo-American opinion and more particularly with French opinion, of which he characteristically speaks with cold hostility and disdain.

In the essay, "On Pasternak Soberly," Milosz is ready to think that time brings in its revenges; that the haughtily bohemian poet pays for his haughtiness by losing his public; "Yet the poet has to pay the price: there are limits beyond which he could not go and maintain communication with his readers. Few are connoisseurs. Sophistication . . . is self-perpetuating like drug addiction." All very well. Yet the fact is that, so long as Pasternak appeared before the public only as a lyrist, he could be tolerated, even in the Soviet Union, and could "maintain communication with his readers." Only when, in his novel, Pasternak engaged with *le langage scientifique* as well as *le langage lyrique,* did he fall foul of the Soviet regime, and thereby lose his readers. It is not at all clear that Milosz has ever taken the force of the painful irony: so long as the poet, East or West, appears before the public only as a lyrist, banking on the irresponsibilities traditionally associated with that role, he will be tolerated by the governing class and allowed to communicate with his readers; it is when he oversteps that pariah's privilege that he is in trouble. That access to *le langage scientifique* which Milosz insisted on, so as to keep communications open with a more than "poetry-reading" public, is most likely to close those avenues of communication, even with "poetry-readers." Milosz is not a popular poet, and never will be; precisely for those reasons that first impelled him to seek a wider audience. So long as readers, alike in the free and the unfree worlds, conceive of the poet as lyrist, so long will a poet who refuses the lyrical contract fail to find readers, or else lose those he has already found.

MILOSZ'S DEPARTURE FROM LYRIC

I have suggested, going for support to the writings of Milosz, that no concerned and ambitious poet of the present-day, aware of the enormities of twentieth-century history, can for long remain content with the privileged irresponsibility allowed to, or imposed on, the *lyric* poet. This is not a contention that will be readily accepted; for less earnest poets are grateful for this privilege, and jealous of it, and their publics are ready to ensure it for them, since it absolves the reader from ever taking his poets' sentiments to heart, except as the poignant expression of a momentary mood.

The most august and canonical text normally cited, to validate this diminution of all poetry to the lyric, is an eloquent passage from Keats's letters:

> I had not a dispute but a disquisition with Dilke, on various subjects; several things dovetailed in my mind, and at once it struck me, what a quality went to form a Man of Achievement especially in Literature and which Shakespeare possessed so enormously—I mean *Negative Capability,* that is when man is capable of being in uncertainties, Mysteries, doubts, without any irritable reaching after fact and reason. Coleridge, for instance, would let go by a fine isolated verisimilitude caught from the Penetralium of mystery, from being incapable of remaining content with half knowledge. This pursued through Volumes would perhaps take us no further than this, that with a great poet the sense of beauty overcomes every other consideration, or rather obliterates all consideration.

Milosz as we have seen, speaking of his own poem "No More," refuses to remain content with this Keatsian consolation—"beauty at best" is what he says he achieved in that poem of his, plainly implying that, so far as he is concerned, that is not enough.

Accordingly it is interesting that in a symposium on Milosz a few years ago (*Ironwood,* 18), the participants disagreed about how far, if at all, Milosz's procedures could be justified by this Keatsian standard. To Marisha Chamberlain it seemed clear that "he possesses that characteristic that Keats called 'negative capability,' which distinguishes the great artist: the ability to stand in doubt for a long time, to proceed from failed attempt to failed attempt, keeping alive the appetite for the problem itself." To Mark Rudman on the other hand, it seemed that "maybe the best way to put it is that Milosz has rejected a concept that has formed the basis of romantic poetry, 'negative capability,' to which poets who might not agree on anything else often cleave." So far as Rudman was concerned, this was an unavoidable implication, seeing that "Milosz writes in the first person a poetry of statement and, with some irony, is willing to address us all, a generalized or ideal-typical other, abjuring metaphors and riddles—anything that can be construed as poetic device, and demands of himself a lucidity so that he can't be mistaken." Rudman is surely wrong in detail; for, as we saw from Milosz's comments on his own poem "No More," there is in poetry no way to abjure "anything that can be construed as poetic device." Still, as will be gathered from the tenor of my argument so far, I am sure that by and large Mark Rudman is right on this large issue, and Marisha Chamberlain is wrong: Milosz is not a Keatsian poet, is not prepared to be.

In this symposium a more ambitious essay than either Chamberlain's or Rudman's is "Reading Milosz" by Robert Hass. This must be attended to more closely, if only because Hass has shown himself to be among the most accomplished and resourceful of Milosz's translators. But Hass's essay lets us in for some new problems, since it is centrally concerned with Milosz's development as a poet, or rather with a crucial phase of that development. Moreover Hass supplies dates for four long poems, three of them in *Selected Poems* and one in *Bells in Winter*; and I shall suppose, in view of Hass's close cooperation with Milosz, that these dates are authoritative. In any case we must, at whatever risk, engage with Robert Hass's argument. And in the first place he is surely right to see a crucial watershed in Milosz's development in his discovery, apparently some time in the 1950s, of the crucial importance to him of the writings of the Frenchwoman Simone Weil, of whom he wrote in 1960 that she was "at least by temperament, an Albigensian, a Cathar; this is the key to her thought." Milosz's admiration for Weil is intimated in *Emperor of the Earth,* and underlined in the Charles Eliot Norton lectures.

Hass accordingly suggests, in a way that falls in very agreeably with my own findings, that what Milosz needed in order to lay aside the polemics of the nineteen-fifties and to explore the suggestions of Simone Weil was "a more ample form than the individual lyric." And Milosz found this first, so Hass suggests, in "Album of Dreams" (1959). Certainly this poem — painstakingly structured as a journal of dreams, each entry dated, from May 10 of one year through to April 3 of the next — is thus at great pains to assert that its form is anything but "organic." On the other hand it may be thought to be, as a whole, tedious. Robert Hass finds: "There is a freedom in the movement of this poem, in its collage of clashing elements. . . ." But the freedom, some of us will think, is of that ultimately or quite immediately tedious sort wherein "anything goes":

> When slowly, in that complete stillness
> not even the rustle of a lizard disturbed,
> we heard gravel crunch under the truck wheels
> and saw, suddenly, standing on a hill
> a pink corset with fluttering ribbons.
> Further on, a second and a third. So, baring our heads,
> we walked towards them, temples in ruins.

For Robert Hass this is "a Bunuel- or Magritte-like marriage of the Waste-land to eros and time." But if we find nothing potently erotic in pink corsets, we surely register not freedom but the gratuitous, the arbitrary. The irrationality of dreams has been so far indulged that the rationality which we ask of art has been denied us. In responding so, do we convict ourselves of that "irritable reaching after fact and reason" which Keats judged inimical to poetry? I think not.

Thus we seem to find, on the evidence of poems available to us in English, that when Milosz felt a need for " a more ample form than the individual lyric," his first gropings after such a form were unsuccessful. We could hardly expect anything else. The 1960 sequence, "From the Chronicles of the Town of Pornic," seems to be also unsuccessful, though in a different way. The trouble here seems to be not the unlimited and therefore boring freedom of the dream, but on the contrary excessively servile adherence to the historical record. (We are however judging this on inadequate evidence; only four of its sections have been translated.)

The next two attempts at ample form seem to have been

"Throughout Our Lands" (1961) and "Bobo's Metamorphosis" (1962). The lands said to be "ours" in 1961 are, for the first time, unequivocally of the New World; Milosz writes as one newly arrived in California, and along with undeniably American locations (as in the fine Section five, which seems to be set on Lake Tahoe), there appear Old World figures transplanted to the New, Father Junipero Serra and Cabeza de Vaca. Plainly one section of the poem after another would profit by being set beside passages from Milosz's *Visions from San Francisco Bay*; but those prose essays come several years later, and it is legitimate to wonder if in 1961 Milosz had had time to become sufficiently inward with the new terrain, to depend upon it so heavily as he does in "Throughout Our Lands."

"Bobo's Metamorphosis" is a great deal more brilliant and assured. It must have been particularly in Robert Hass's mind when he observed, very justly and instructively (*Ironwood*, 165): "Milosz requires the open forms not just to express a collage of different attitudes toward experience, but for the rather startling shifts in scale and perspective." Hass points out that some of these shifts produce effects that can rightly be called "Swiftian." But along with these scatological transformations are others of a quite different, more radiant cast:

> I was hovering at each flower from the day of creation,
> I knocked on the closed doors of the beaver's halls and the
> mole's. . . .

Or:

> An acrid dust was falling from flexible columns inside cin-
> nabar flowers.

Or again, there is the beautifully tender and witty variation on a famous *topos* from that ancient poem of transformations, Ovid's *Metamorphoses*:

> Stars of Philemon, stars of Baucis,
> Above their house entangled by the roots of an oak
> And a wandering god, soundly asleep on a thong-strung bed,
> His fist for a pillow.
> An advancing weevil encounters his sandal
> And pushes on painfully through a foot-polished mesa.

In this imaginative identification with the microscopic scale of "the green world" as insects know it, Milosz may remind the English-speaking reader less of Swift than of Swift's contemporary and friend, the greater poet Alexander Pope. In any case, these abrupt contractions and expansions occur not just in the spatial dimension but also, perhaps more affectingly for most readers, in the dimension of time:

> My eyes closed, I was grown up and small. . . .

Or again:

> At a swing she pulls up her skirt
> To do indecent things with me or her cousin,
> And all of a sudden she walks grayhaired in the scraggy suburb,
> Then departs without delay where all the maidens go.

Human consciousness is confined neither by the spatial axis of meters and hectares, nor by the temporal axis of clocks and calendars. Hence the identification in Section IV with another great hymn to transformations, Shakespeare's *The Tempest*. And so, although we must take the force of Robert Hass's argument that "Bobo's Metamorphosis," like the other "ample" poems, is written in the shadow of Simone Weil's agonized and stringent witness, yet the overall temper of this poem I would describe as "elated," needing all the witty dryness it can muster so as to describe, without seeming woozy or complacent, its arc from "ecstasy at sunrise" to "Thus were affirmed humanness, tenderness." Thus, we may emphasize . . . thus, and not otherwise — not from the fixed stance of the meditative lyrist, nor with his consistent tone — can humanness and tenderness be affirmed. The didactic thrust, and the quite unKeatsian certainty, seem unmistakable. Accordingly I do not read from this poem what Robert Hass seems to read from it: "ontological vertigo, a deep feeling of dread and wonder at being alive, and there is very little comfort in it, and no resolution." Though indeed and very properly "dread" is constantly present, yet "Bobo's Metamorphosis" brings comfort, both achieves and purveys "resolution."

"City Without a Name" is a long poem in twelve sections, dated as from "Berkeley, 1965." It was unknown in English until 1984 when, in a version by Milosz himself along with Robert Hass, Robert Pinsky, and Renata Gorczynski, it appeared in *The Threepenny Review* (Berkeley) and in *The Separate Notebooks* (Ecco Press). After a first section which supplies the unnamed city with the not unexpected name "Vilno" (rendered, however, emblematically, not literally), the second section reveals that Vilno is being remembered in, and seen through the lens of, California:

> In Death Valley salt gleams from a dried-up lake bed.
> Defend, defend yourself says the tick-tock of the blood.
> From the futility of solid rock, no wisdom.

After five further sections which, though relatively short, reveal the poem as very ambitious (we note for example that Milosz is identifying himself with the most illustrious of his Polish masters, Mickiewicz), we are reminded again in the eighth section that images of his native Lithuania are recalled and recovered through the lens of the American Southwest:

> Absent, burning, acrid, salty, sharp.
> Thus the feast of Insubstantiality.
> Under a gathering of clouds anywhere.
> In a bay, on a plateau, in a dry arroyo.
> No density. No hardness of stone.
> Even the Summa thins into straw and smoke.
> And the angelic choirs sail over in a pomegranate seed.
> Not for us their leisure and the blowing of trumpets.

The difference between "rock" and "stone" seems here hardly significant. And if it is not, then one aspect of the movement through the poem seems to be graphed in the change from "futility" and "no wisdom" associated with stone in Section 2, to the stone's "density" and "hardness" that in Section 8 the speaker yearns for and fails to find. The poem does not rest there, however; and in the sections that remain it is fluid and vegetal rather than lapidary images that command the poet's allegiance and embody as much comfort as he can find.

And this is characteristic: though Milosz is surely a modernist (rather than "post-modernist," whatever that cant term may be thought to mean), there is one important current of international modernism—to be found as it were east of him, in Mandelstam, as well as west of him, in for instance Pound—that is in his work conspicuous by its absence, or else is called into presence only so as to be repudiated. This is the current that we may call "lapidary," of which the classic and originating formulation for modern times was surely Théophile Gautier's, in "L'Art":

> Les dieux eux-mêmes meurent.
> Mais les vers souverains
> Demeurent
> Plus fort que les airains.
>
> Sculpte, lime, cisèle;
> Que ton rêve flottant
> Se scelle
> Dans le bloc résistant!

This Gautieresque ambition after the hard-edged, the chiselled, is seldom noticed by Milosz except with hostility and disdain, as when he speaks of "the products of the jeweler's chisel to which we have become inadvertently accustomed." This comes in an essay called "Carmel," in *Visions from San Francisco Bay,* a piece of writing to which we must now attend rather closely because it represents Milosz's most considered encounter with one of his English-language peers, the Californian poet Robinson Jeffers.

Milosz has written of Jeffers elsewhere, notable in an essay that he published in *The Michigan Quarterly Review* (Summer 1977):

What do I consider reality? Probably not the same thing as an American poet does. I will choose a case which is perhaps extreme, but significant. When I came to California, I dedicated much time to the poetry of Robinson Jeffers. In my opinion he is a poet of great stature, unjustly thrown down into near-oblivion from the pedestal he occupied in the twenties. Jeffers deliberately opposed avant-garde fashions deriving from French Symbolism and, in clear-cut transparent syntax, described in his poems what was for him the most real, the shore of the Pacific near his home in Carmel. And yet, when reading Jeffers, I discovered that those orange-violet sunsets, those flights of pelicans, those fishing boats in the morning fog, as faithfully represented as if they were photographs—all that was for me pure fiction. I said to myself that Jeffers, who professed, as he called it, "inhumanism," took refuge in an artificial world which he invented using ideas taken from biology textbooks and from the philosophy of Nietzsche.

Though Milosz is surely right to remind us of Jeffers's claim upon us, and although we must admire Milosz's generosity and the char-

acteristically independent judgment that takes him to an unfashionable author, all the same the case of Jeffers is not merely, as Milosz
allows, "extreme," it is also wildly unrepresentative, freakish. For
Milosz goes on to define the allegedly non-American reality that his
poetry deals with, as "Poetry and History"—quite as if there were
not American poets who concern themselves with that reality, even
though Robinson Jeffers mostly does not.

In *Visions from San Francisco Bay* the consideration of Jeffers
is far more deliberate, as we see from the arrangement by which the
essay, "Carmel," is sandwiched between one of Jeffers's poems, "Con-
tinent's End," and Milosz's own poem, "To Robinson Jeffers." Moreover Milosz has never done anything better, as English prose, than
this essay; and one marvels at the fact that it was first composed in
Polish, for Polish-speaking readers. Brief though it is, there are few
more beautiful and poignant records of one poet meeting in the spirit
another, saluting him, feeling with him, yet in the end resisting the
hegemony that he seeks to establish. It is the more remarkable that,
as even a casual reader must notice, Milosz misreads the poem by
Jeffers that he quotes in full and then reflects upon. For in "Conti-
nent's End," one of the best of Jeffers's poems, the poet quite explicitly does *not,* as Milosz says he does, see in the ocean "the fullest
incarnation of harmony." On the contrary Jeffers says, addressing
the ocean:

> You were much younger when we crawled out of the
> womb and lay in the sun's eye on the tideline.
>
> It was long and long ago; we have grown proud since then
> and you have grown bitter; life retains
> Your mobile soft unquiet strength; and envies hardness,
> the insolent quietness of stone.
>
> The tides are in our veins, we still mirror the stars, life is
> your child, but there is in me
> Older and harder than life and more impartial, the eye that
> watched before there was an ocean.

And in Jeffers's last lines it is plain that he declares allegiance to
something more ancient than ocean:

> Mother, though my song's measure is like your surf-beat's
> ancient rhythm, I never learned it of you.

> Before there was any water there were tides of fire, both
> our tones flow from the older fountain.

In the light of the positive value that Jeffers gave to stone, alike in
his life as in his art, we may reasonably suppose that among the "tides
of fire" that he here celebrates were those that composed the igne-
ous rocks.

Thus, though we may and must applaud in the essay, "Carmel,"
Milosz's generosity and candor ("But, after all, whatever his faults,
he was truly a great poet"), and although on the other hand we may
endorse Milosz's judgment, at the end of his poem to Jeffers, that
the latter chose to proclaim "an inhuman thing," still there is something skewed and partial in Milosz's apprehension of Jeffers. And
where he goes askew is on the matter of "the stony."

Another misreading or misrepresentation (that turns on the same
issue, the lapidary) is more surprising, yet need not detain us for so
long. In the fifth of his Harvard lectures Milosz considers two Polish
poems, both lapidary in the sense that they are concerned with the
nature of stone as that nature is apprehended by the human imagination. The first of these is Zbigniew Herbert's "The Pebble," on which
Milosz's comments strike me as exemplary. The other example is from
Milosz's friend and Polish contemporary Aleksandr Wat (1900–1967),
whose *Mediterranean Poems,* edited and translated by Milosz himself, appeared in 1977. Milosz says that in Wat's poetry "inanimate
nature becomes an object of envy." And in the verses from Wat that
he quotes to validate this, the type and instance of enviably inanimate nature is *stone*:

> With the eyes of a stone, myself
> a stone among stones, and like them sensitive,
> pulsating to the turning of the sun. Retreating into
> the depths of myself, stone,
> motionless, silent; growing cold; present through a waning
> of presence—in the cold
> attractions of the moon. Like sand diminishing in
> an hourglass, evenly,
> Ceaselessly, uniformly, grain by grain. Thus I shall be submitted
> only to the rhythms of day and night. But—
> no dance in them, no whirling, no frenzy: only
> monastic rule and silence.

> They do not become, they are. Nothing else. Nothing
>   else, I thought, loathing
> all which becomes.

But this is to stop short in Section 2 of Wat's extraordinary "Songs of a Wanderer." By Section 4 of that poem the speaker has seen through the illusion that stone, in its constancy, its density and hardness, possesses or may symbolize for the human observer a minimal integrity that can be for him a mainstay and a moral talisman. On the contrary:

> It is not erosion which crumbles stone
>   here. For the rot
> is in its nature. To rot, to scale off, to disintegrate: this
>   is posited in the law
> of minerals. In the law of mollusks. In the law of man.

What is impressive and disconcerting about Wat's corrosive treatment of this theme is that it is conducted, as the poem itself makes clear and as is emphasized by the poet's notes, in a quite specific stonescape, that of the Préalpes de Grasse in southern France. With this in mind we must suppose that Wat quite intentionally subjected to scrutiny, and found wanting, the whole mediterranean or "classic" culture that through the centuries centered itself on stonework, on the marmoreal, in sculpture and architecture most notably. (To be sure, the distinct and seemingly opposed tradition of Ovidian metamorphosis is "mediterranean" no less.)

However that may be, the mere possibility brings into high relief how indifferent Milosz has been to this powerful strain not just in international modernism but in the entire cultural inheritance of the West. If he has stood on Mediterranean shores, or moved through the stonescapes of Florence and Rome and Sulmona, such experiences have left little or no mark on his poetry. In the essay, "Carmel," he chides Jeffers for having introduced, in the tower he built with his own hands at Carmel, a touch of pseudo-Gothic: "Why didn't he maintain the stone's inherent modesty all the way through?" But in my reading of Milosz this discrimination about worked stone is the exception that proves the rule. Usually when Milosz looks for images of permanence he finds them in rural, not in civic scenes, in the arboreal and the vegetal rather than in masonry. If this impression is accurate, it means that we have in Milosz not altogether a distinctly *northern* sensibility (for some North European cities—St. Petersburg and Amsterdam, London and Edinburgh—have been celebrated by their poets as images of the civic made monumental in worked stone), but a sensibility of the northern *woodlands*. In "City Without a Name," Vilno is clearly not a city in any sense that precludes its being merely a distended village. Milosz circles around, and would like to come to rest on, the village in a forest-clearing: and when he fantasizes about what he does when he handles words, he sees himself as whittling and carving timber, not quarrying and then chiseling marble. The last lines of his poem "To Robinson Jeffers" are from this point of view characteristic and telling:

> Better to carve suns and moons on the joints of crosses
> as was done in my district. To birches and firs
> give feminine names. To implore protection
> against the mute and treacherous might
> than to proclaim, as you did, an inhuman thing.

The stony is "inhuman." This isn't quite what Milosz says or implies, and so we cannot with certainty impute the sentiment to him. But it's a persistent unexamined assumption among dwellers in northern latitudes, including English-speakers. And Milosz's imagination moves along tracks so closely parallel that in this respect his achievement for good or ill may find ready acceptance among the North Americans and the British. He is nearer to Natty Bumppo than he imagines; and he is an Ovidian poet, celebrating metamorphosis and flux.

Although "Bobo's Metamorphosis" includes passages more brilliant, and more brilliantly affecting, than anything in "City Without a Name," the latter poem is less mannered, mellower and more humane. What both poems show is that Milosz has overcome the seeming necessity to choose between writing of his lost Europe and writing of his new-found California. Both worlds are now, and will be hereafter, folded together in his writing so that each takes on salience and meaning in reflected light from the other. It is this surely—the layering or laminating of one historical actuality on to or into another—that makes it possible, and necessary, to declare Milosz a (perhaps belated) "modernist." From this time forward he will be a Californian poet to just the extent that he is still a Polish/Lithuanian poet, and vice-versa. As early as 1942, in a poem called "A Book in the

Ruins" (in *The Separate Notebooks,* translated by Milosz and Robert Hass), he had seen that this was how it would have to be:

> Only when two times, two forms are drawn
> Together and their legibility
> Disturbed, do you see that immortality
> Is not very different from the present
> And is for its sake.

It would take another twenty years at least before this declared necessity of a double perspective could be transformed from a precept or a fleeting perception into habitual experience and so into a necessary principle of poetic structuring. Such double perspective or doubled focus need not issue in irony; and in Milosz it seldom does so, except incidentally. But it is plainly incompatible with the single singing voice of the lyric.

We thus come round to press again the insufficiency of the lyric mode for registering, except glancingly, the complexity of twentieth-century experience. Since I have invoked, as spokesman for the lyric voice, a figure so illustrious and never to be discounted as John Keats, it is worthwhile pointing out that in our time an anti-Keatsian position is to be found articulated by persons not much less distinguished. Here for instance, surprisingly, is Pasternak, writing in his own English to his American translator Eugene Kayden, in 1958:

> You say I am "first and last a poet, a lyric poet." Is it really so? And should I feel proud of being just that? And do you realize the meaning of my being no more than that, whereas it hurts me to feel that I have not had the ability to express in greater fullness the whole of poetry and life in their complete unity?

From farther back in time, and from the heart of English-speaking culture, comes another voice. This is the Anglo-Irish painter J.B. Yeats, in 1906 writing about Swinburne to his son the poet, William Butler Yeats:

> More than thirty years ago I heard many stories of Swinburne—amongst others of his reciting his ode to Mazzini himself, and often bursting into floods of tears. A capacity for nervous weeping is exactly what I should expect from his kind of lyrism. I also heard he used to say in conversation that he and Shelley were the only great

poets because they alone were gentlemen. Where again he comes up to expectation—yet to be a poet it needs more than that you be an aristocratic cad even tho' you have in addition Greek and Latin, an Oxford education and a gift of language that is like the sea for strength and copiousness. Out of these you may make a lyrist, granted a gift for musical speech you can make that sort of poet *out of anything.*

To be a poet in the true and great sense of the word needs much more. It is *quite possible to be lyrical and not poetical*—to be a poet it is necessary first of all to be a man. The high vitality and vivid experience, the impulses, doings and sufferings of a Tolstoi, a Shakespeare or a Dante,—all are needed.

Unless I have wholly misunderstood Czeslaw Milosz, he would agree with this passionate restatement of an old truth. Tolstoy, Shakespeare, Dante—that is the company he aspires to keep, and it is by the awesomely demanding standards of that company that he asks to be judged.

MILOSZ AND THE DITHYRAMB

The pristine and definitive form of lyric is the song; and the singer of a song is not on oath. The sentiment and opinion expressed in a song by Robert Burns are to be understood as true only for as long as the singing lasts. They are true only to that occasion and that mood; we shall not be disconcerted if the next song contradicts that first one. The same holds true of less song-like lyrists, like those among Burns's near-contemporaries who, in Hugh Kenner's words, "were accustomed to take up a stance in a particularized landscape and meditate." The Gray of the famous *Elegy* and even the Wordsworth of "Tintern Abbey" are similarly not on oath; what they say in their poems is to be understood as true only to that scene and that occasion—a scene and an occasion which are accordingly particularized quite scrupulously. Of course analogous scenes and occasions are or may be part of the experience of every thoughtful reader; and he may well feel that the poets have articulated with great purity the sentiments that such scenes and occasions have inspired in him. And thus we may feel that the sentiments expressed by Gray and Keats and Wordsworth are those "to which every bosom returns an echo." When this happens we respond all the more poignantly and gratefully because of the poets' modesty in offering their musings as not having any such universal validity. But there may be, and have been, poets who, under the pressure of historical experience, find it impossible to appear before the public thus modestly. I am suggesting that Milosz is such an immodest poet, as was (quite notoriously) Ezra Pound.

Yet if in this way we begin to see in Milosz a poet distrustful of, and refusing to be restricted to, such lyrical purity, the last fifteen pages of his *Selected Poems* (1980) are disconcerting. For first in these pages comes "Dithyramb," a short poem which by that title may seem to claim lyric status. Moreover the same dithyrambic mode is maintained in three of the four poems which remain in the volume, and is sustained throughout the poem in eleven sections, "With Trumpets and Zithers," which concludes—and crowns, for it is very impressive—a book that obviously was planned by Milosz with some care. Indeed it must be said that if there were not other evidence to be taken account of, a careful reader of *Selected Poems* would have every right to see, in its author, a poet who conquered an initial distrust of the lyric voice so as to break through in the end to speaking in just that voice—in the specially emphatic and full-throated lyric tone that we call "dithyrambic."

It is notable however that in these last pages of *Selected Poems,* one poem often retorts to or even contradicts its predecessor. To my mind the most pregnant and instructive of these "pairings" is in the two poems which precede "Dithyramb." They are "On Angels" and "The Master." The first of these, a beautifully spare and tentative though witty poem, shares its central trope—of "angels" as "messengers"—with a poem that Aleksandr Wat addressed to Milosz, which figures in Milosz's translation as section eight of Wat's "Dreams from the Shore of the Mediterranean." Milosz's poem advances with touching hesitancy a view of the poet's, the artist's, role as radically and radiantly innocent. "The Master," the companion-piece which follows, insists contrariwise on the artist's complicity with evil, that complicity being the price that he pays for his mastery:

> No one knows how I was paying. Ridiculous, they believe
> It may be got for nothing. . . .

"The Master" accordingly ends with a harshly sardonic reference to that angelic status which the previous poem had humbly aspired to for the artist:

> A language of angels! Before you mention Grace
> Mind that you do not deceive yourself and others.
> What comes from my evil—that only is true . . .

—where the evil, I suppose, is not just original sin but the masterful presumption incurred by the artist when he achieves, or in order to achieve, mastery. At any rate, this pairing of affirmation with retort or rejoinder, "On Angels" with "The Master," should ensure that when we hear the dithyrambic voice of "With Trumpets and Zithers" we

43

do not forget how that voice may be very far from innocent, angelic, a voice of personal or civic rightness.

One would be less likely to make that mistake after reading what Nietzsche says of the dithyramb in his *Birth of Tragedy,* where he insists that the archaic dithyramb out of which Greek tragedy developed is essentially different from all other forms of the choric ode, just as the poet-musician of the dithyramb is essentially different from the rhapsode.

Milosz once suggested that Americans in particular often misread Nietzsche. This was in an essay on Henry Miller, in *Visions from San Francisco Bay,* where Milosz is at his most haughtily European:

> Something disturbing occurs when Americans throw themselves on European authors, especially Nietzsche. The play of their contradictions disappears, a certain trait of humor hidden beneath their fury, which only the historical imagination provides, whereas what the Americans extract are the elements which allow them reconciliation with the ideal of the "natural man"; actually, the man of the natural sciences. Nietzsche, an unhappy Lucifer, proud and pure, found plebeian incarnation in Miller. As some one has remarked, fornication is the poetry of the masses. Miller brings no glad tidings, no *gaia scienza* to a humanity which he condemns to incipient chaos, meaninglessness, and, finally, extermination.

Milosz's tone here is unattractive. And there are other things wrong with this essay:

> Henry Miller was so extreme in opposing his own person to everything outside of it that he rejected literature as a collection of inherited patterns, in order to stand unique, to say a Mass to himself, to present the image of himself as a perfect male. (Whitman, Hart Crane, Ezra Pound, Hemingway, all wrote "songs of themselves.") To me, that Miller seemed like a medium in a trance.

Whitman and Crane and Pound and Hemingway—each is a distinct "case," and they are getting less than justice when they are herded together in one peremptory parenthesis. All the same this essay must be consulted when we ask what Milosz intended by introducing the seemingly lyric voice at the end of *Selected Poems* under the challenging and highly specific rubric, "Dithyramb." For there are places in these last pages where we hear a note that might reasonably be called "Whitmanesque":

On many shores at once I am lying cheek in the sand and
the same ocean runs in, beating its ecstatic drums.

Are we to suppose that whatever Milosz had said, or was to say, in
his essay on Henry Miller, at the time he wrote these poems the European expatriate had Americanized himself to the point where he could
emulate and echo "Song of Myself"? Obviously this is a question
of the greatest importance, if we are to understand him.

It is here that Nietzsche helps. In the first place I take it that the
very title, "With Trumpets and Zithers" (even, it may be, the naming
of those musical instruments rather than others), can be rightly glossed
out of Section 2 of *The Birth of Tragedy*:

> The music of Apollo was Doric architectonics in tone, but in tones
> that were merely suggestive, such as those of the cithara. The very
> element which forms the essence of Dionysian music (and hence of
> music in general) is carefully excluded as un-Apollinian—namely, the
> emotional power of the tone, the uniform flow of the melody, and the
> utterly incomparable world of harmony. In the Dionysian dithyramb
> man is incited to the greatest exaltation of all his symbolic faculties;
> something never before experienced struggles for utterance—the anni-
> hilation of the veil of *maya,* oneness as the soul of the race and of
> nature itself. The essence of nature is now to be expressed symboli-
> cally; we need a new world of symbols; and the entire symbolism of
> the body is called into play, not the mere symbolism of the lips, face
> and speech but the whole pantomime of dancing, forcing every mem-
> ber into rhythmic movement. Then the other symbolic powers sud-
> denly press forward, particularly those of music, in rhythmics, dynam-
> ics, and harmony. To grasp this collective release of all the symbolic
> powers, man must have already attained that height of self-abnegation
> which seeks to express itself symbolically through all these powers—
> and so the dithyrambic votary of Dionysus is understood only by his
> peers.   (translated by Walter Kaufmann)

In this rather windy passage what is signalled by "that height of self-
abnegation" is developed by Nietzsche later (Section 5) so as to put
the dithyramb, as he conceived of it, at the opposite extreme from
any "Song of Myself." Speaking with a confidence that was already
unwarranted in his own time, and has had less and less warrant in
the years since, the youthful Nietzsche, echoing the accents of his
first master Schopenhauer, declares in Section 5:

> we know the subjective artist only as the poor artist, and throughout the entire range of art we demand first of all the conquest of the subjective, redemption from the "ego," and the silencing of the individual will and desire; indeed, we find it impossible to believe in any truly artistic production, however insignificant, if it is without objectivity, without pure contemplation devoid of interest.

If this could not confidently be asserted of any actual "we" in 1872, still less can it be posited in the 1980s. Now it is very far from true that "we know the subjective artist only as the poor artist." But we have found reason for thinking that by Milosz at any rate this position might be enthusiastically endorsed. He wrote in *The Captive Mind*: "I am not in favor of art that is too subjective. My poetry has always been a means of checking on myself." Accordingly to him, and to us if we want to sympathize with him, there is abundant point to the question which Nietzsche, proceeding from that position, poses to himself:

> Hence our aesthetics must first solve the problem of how the "lyrist" is possible as an artist—he who, according to the experience of all ages, is continually saying "I" and running through the entire chromatic scale of his passions and desires.

To Nietzsche, the precocious Professor of Classical Philology, this question took the form of how to explain why the Ancients habitually put on a par Homer, the supremely Apollinian (or Apollonian) artist, and the vehemently "I"-saying lyrist, Archilochus. For us the problem is how to explain, in the case of Milosz, so opposed to the poet's writing "a Mass to himself," the frequent appearance of the first person singular in his poetry generally, and particularly in "With Trumpets and Zithers."

Nietzsche's solution can also be ours. Maintaining that "the artist has already surrendered his subjectivity in the Dionysian process," Nietzsche argues:

> The "I" of the lyrist therefore sounds from the depths of his being: its "subjectivity," in the sense of modern aestheticians, is a fiction. When Archilochus, the first Greek lyrist, proclaims to the daughters of Lycambes both his mad love and his contempt, it is not his passion alone that dances before us in orgiastic frenzy; but we see Dionysus and the Maenads, we see the drunken reveler Archilochus sunk down

in slumber—as Euripides depicts it in the *Bacchae,* the sleep on the high mountain pasture, in the noonday sun.

It is from this point of view that we may scrutinize the "I" of "With Trumpets and Zithers." And in the first place we note that "I" often appears in contexts that negate it. Section 4 is a clear instance:

> Nothing but laughter and weeping. Terror and no defense
> and arm in arm they drag me to a pit of tangled bones.
> Soon I will join their dance, with bailiffs, wenches and kings,
> such as they used to paint on the tablecloth at our revels.
> With a train of my clock carried by the Great Jester, not I,
> just the Sinner to whom a honey-sweet age was brought
> by winged Fortune.
> To whom three masked Slavic devils, Duliban, Kostruban,
> Mendrela, squealing and farting, would offer huge
> smoking plates.
> Fingers grabbing at fingers, tongues fornicating with tongues,
> but not mine was the sense of touch, not mine was the
> knowledge.
> Beyond seven rocky mountains I searched for my Teacher and
> yet I am here, not myself, at a pit of tangled bones.
> I am standing on a theatrum, astonished by the last things,
> the puppet Death has black ribs and still I cannot believe.

The "I" that appears in the second verset is promptly cancelled ("not I") in the third; the knowledge and the touch announced in the fifth verset are declared to be "not mine"; and in the penultimate verset we are told, "I am here, not myself." In the last verset the word "theatrum," unknown to the *Shorter O.E.D.,* appears to be a latinization of the Greek *theātron,* defined in *The Oxford Companion to Classical Literature* as "circular tiers of seats, generally cut out of the side of a hill"—a physical feature of ancient Greek theatres which Nietzsche makes much of, to support his contention that "there was at bottom no opposition between public and chorus; everything is merely a great sublime chorus of dancing and singing satyrs or of those who permit themselves to be represented by such satyrs." The voice that utters the dithyramb is as far as possible from being a personal voice, the voice of an individual; just as the minds of those on the *theātron* who mutely participate are, at that moment, as far as possible from being the minds of individual mere spectators.

It is only by conceiving along these lines how the individual can be parted from his consciousness, that we can understand the bold assumption made in the brilliant second section, that it is meaningful for an "I" to address its own consciousness:

> I address you, my consciousness, when in a sultry night shot
>   with lightnings the plane is landing at Beauvais or
>   Kalamazoo.
> And a stewardess moves about quietly so not to wake anyone
>   while the cellular wax of cities glimmers beneath.
> I believed I would understand but it is late and I know
>   nothing except laughter and weeping.
> The wet grasses of fertile deltas cleaned me from time and
>   changed all into a present without beginning or end.
> I disappear in architectural spirals, in lines of a crystal, in the
>   sound of instruments playing in forests. . . .

A "me" that is "cleaned . . . from time and changed all into a present without beginning or end" was not readily nor easily available to a poet, Milosz, who had, in *Native Realm* and elsewhere, resolved to write a poetry that would always "contain history." Again the question arises: how was that attainable by Milosz, except at the price of surrender to the overweening lyrical "I" that he had always distrusted? And the answer seems to be: by way of the dithyrambic "I," which is not overweening because not in any way personal. The dithyrambic mode, if Nietzsche was right about it, allows the modern poet to participate in orgiastic release, in crowd-awareness, at the same time as he maintains his distance from it, structuring and thereby chastening it inside what is, in modern times, an archaic *genre*. At the risk of being repetitious we cannot help but note how different it is, thus to specify no particular scene and occasion, or else to bury such specification deep within the poem, from the procedure of the meditative lyric as we have known it since Gray or Wordsworth or Bryant or Keats, in which the speaker establishes the scene and the occasion from the start, stationing himself so that whatever meditations he may indulge or may be prompted to shall be understood as valid, as true, as "what he will stand over," only in that specified context both of time and place. That, quite clearly, is not the procedure of the dithyramb.

I do not pretend that I can present an exegesis of "With Trumpets and Zithers" as a whole. Undoubtedly, the dithyrambic convention

once established, Milosz in places permits himself an "I "that is personal, the voice of a man born in Polish Lithuania in 1911. Section 5
is one place where this happens, and another is Section 8—a splen-
did evocation of what Milosz could see from a Berkeley window any
summer morning, the high fog burning off all over San Francisco
Bay. Elsewhere, however, there is renewed emphasis on an "I" that
is not an individualized "I":

> The "I" is felt with amazement in the heartbeat, but so large it cannot
> be filled by the whole Earth with her seasons.

It is worth reflecting that the discriminating admirer of Whitman
might want to make the same dissociations inside Whitman's "I" also.

A particular problem arises with Sections 6 and 7. Stanislaw Baranczak in a valuable article (*Parnassus,* Spring/Summer 1982) has
quoted from both these sections, to support his contention that "Like
many other poets [Milosz] is tormented by the immutable shortcom-
ing of language: its being out of proportion to reality. On the one
hand, language has many different names for the same thing; on the
other, it is insufficient in relation to the abundance of the real world."
There is no doubt Baranczak is right to say that Milosz worries the
hoary "problem of universals," and Baranczak is helpful when he
sends us to a poem much earlier in *Selected Poems,* "Throughout
our Lands." There Milosz acts out the nominalist/realist dilemma,
trying and failing to express the quiddity of one particular reality,
a *pear,* by pointing to it with words that necessarily signify only categories of pear:

> And the word revealed out of darkness was: pear.
> I hovered around it hopping or trying my wings.
> But whenever I was just about to drink its sweetness, it withdrew.
> So I tried Anjou—then a garden's corner,
> Scaling white paint of wooden shutters,
> a dogwood bush and rustling of departed people.
> So I tried Comice—then right away fields
> beyond this (not another) palisade, a brook, countryside.
> So I tried Jargonelle, Bosc and Bergamot.
> No good. Between me and pear, equipages, countries.
> And so I have to live, with this spell on me.

(Not only do "Anjou" and "Comice" fail to pin-point the quiddity
that the poet wants to register, each of the words insists on playing

over, or dredging from his memories, things that for his current purposes are irrelevant—wooden shutters, a palisade, a brook.) Plainly
the speaker is in the same bind in Section 7 of "With Trumpets and
Zithers," at a point where he tries to summon up a particular fox
encountered in his boyhood, and insists vainly:

> Not a general one, a plenipotentiary of the idea of the fox,
>   in his cloak lined with the universals.

On the other hand we need to notice how this discussion of a philosophical crux is introduced. We embark upon it with these lines:

> What separates, falls. Yet my scream "no!" is still heard
>   though it burned out in the wind.
> Only what separates does not fall. All the rest is beyond
>   persistence.
> I wanted to describe this, not that, basket of vegetables. . . .

This surely means on the one hand what Baranczak indicates—that
the separating out of one thing from all others of its class is a project
that can only fall silent, since it is of the nature of language not to
work that way. To name is necessarily to fall to generalizing and clas-
sifying, for that is just what naming is (when we think about it). But
on the other hand "what separates" can equally be understood of
a person who separates himself from his people, from those who share
his language. To do that is to fall, if not into silence, at least into
very imperfect speech, imperfectly communicating with those whose
speech is different. Thus "what separates, falls." And yet, in certain
circumstances, *not* to thus separate from the herd or the tribe is to
fall into dishonour—in ways that we know about from, for instance,
Milosz's novel, *The Seizure of Power*. And thus, "only what separates does not fall." In this way, when we hear the screamed "no!"
that burned out in the wind, what we hear is on the one hand the
"no!" of the nominalist vainly attempting not to generalize, but also
we hear, surely, the "no!" that Milosz cried to communist Poland
when he went into voluntary and permanent exile in 1951. What is
true of the sort of human behavior that we call "utterance" turns out
to be equally, or at least analogously, true of kinds of human behavior that we think of as quite different. How quirky and unreliable
language is (though of course we have nothing to put in its place)
is illustrated with witty audacity a few lines later, when the appar-

ently simple name "cat" is twisted from designating a domestic pet into designating a historically recorded human being called Fénelon:

> No one cares that precisely this cat wrote *The Adventures of Telemachus* . . .

—where the expression is like "a cool cat," in the idiom of hippies and hipsters of the 1960s and perhaps the 1980s.

It cannot be pretended that with these considerations we have cleared away all the problems of "With Trumpets and Zithers." There are places in the poem where, if only because of the permissiveness of its structural unit, the gathering and leaping *verset,* we may be forgiven for finding what Milosz had reprehended in Mayakovsky: "words used as an unshackled vital force." And the first person singular remains elusive and problematic even in the last lines:

> I wanted to be a judge but those whom I called "they" have
> changed into myself.
> I was getting rid of my faith so as not to be better than men and
> women who are certain only of their unknowing.
> And on the roads of my terrestrial homeland turning round
> with the music of the spheres
> I thought that all I could do would be done better one day.

The "I" or "myself" spoken of in these lines remains questionable— is it the individual Milosz, born on such and such a date to such and such a national and/or ethnic identity? Or is it the non-individualized dithyrambic "I" that has spoken from time to time earlier in the poem? The question is important and troublesome because it is tied up with the question of what silent rejoinder we should make to the testimonies, "I wanted . . . I was getting rid of . . . I thought. . . ." Should we respond, "And how wrong you were," or alternatively, "And perhaps you were right"? I would have some sympathy with a reader who should confess himself dissatisfied at being left with such a large uncertainty. If I am not myself dissatisfied, it is because I identify the speaker of the poem with the speaker of "On Angels" but also of "The Master." From the latter poem, it will be remembered, we read a warning not to take the poet or any other artist as *innocent.* In other words, if the poet of "With Trumpets and Zithers" should himself be dubious about how to justify the enterprise that with that poem he found himself launched upon, and should mirror that dubiety in the unanswered questions he leaves us with, I find that not only acceptable but instructive. After all, Nietzsche's whole account of the dithyramb is to the effect that it is pre-moral, expressing a state of mind and feeling in which questions of moral and civic duty are not suspended, since on the contrary they have not yet arisen. Certainly such experiences are not unfamiliar to Milosz. In *The Captive Mind,* for instance, he tells how the memory comes back to him of a twenty-year-old Jewish girl seen as she was shot down by the S.S. in a Warsaw street:

> This girl was not the first nor the last of the millions who were killed when the life-force within them was at its height. But the obstinacy with which this image returns—and always when I am drunk with the beauty of being alive amidst living human beings—merits some reflection. This is perhaps a matter that belongs to the same sphere as do the collective sex orgies of some primitive tribes. At such times, this or another object of desire are the same, all men and women are fused by a great feeling of communion through which everyone belongs to all. Monogamy can give no outlet to such urges. In other words, this is a profound basis for love of mankind, a love one cannot conceive of if, looking at a group of laughing women, one does not recall this young Jewish girl as *one of them,* as identical and ever present.

If we have experienced states of such undifferentiated erotic excitement and pleasure—and who of us has not?—we may think that the dithyrambic experience, or the possibility of it in all its dubiousness, is not after all archaically primitive but available to us in the here and now.

It is interesting that in conceiving of the dithyramb as a fundamentally non-lyrical or at least non-subjective mode, Nietzsche was drawing immediately on Schopenhauer. For Schopenhauer's ideas on art are explicitly adduced and seemingly approved in "A Mirrored Gallery," the first of Milosz's "Separate Notebooks," dated from Berkeley 1977–1979. Here the poet, or rather a *persona* called "The Wanderer," addresses Schopenhauer directly:

> It is easy to guess why you were not liked and never will be. No one had ever so forcefully opposed the child and the genius to the rest of them, always under the power of blind will, of which the essence is

sexual desire; no one has ever so forcefully explained the genius of children; they are onlookers, avid, gluttonous, minds not yet caught by the will of the species, though I would add, led too by Eros, but an Eros who is still free and dances, knowing nothing of goals and service. And the gift of the artist or philosopher likewise has its secret in a hidden hostility toward the earth of the adults. Your language— O philosopher— so logical and precise in its appearance, disguised more than it concealed, so they really had no access to you. Admit it, your only theme was time: a masque on midsummer night, young girls in bloom, ephemerid generations born and dying in a single hour. You asked only one question— is it worthy of man to be seduced and caught?

There are aspects of this passage— for instance, the connecting of the artist's vision with the child's— which may seem, in a disabling sense, "Romantic." But we should take account of Bryan Magee, in his *Philosophy of Schopenhauer* (1983):

Schopenhauer's theory of art . . . is not one that sees art as expression of emotion, or indeed as self-expression of any kind. This is one of the many reasons why it is uncomprehending to think of him as a romantic philosopher (the notion of art as expression of emotion being central to Romanticism). To make an elementary logical point, the fact that our emotions are deeply moved by something does not mean that the purpose of that something is to move our emotions— no one, I take it, would contend that the beauties of nature are vehicles of emotional expression. Great art is great by virtue of its insight into, and its truthfulness to, something other than the artist: the fact that it moves us *and, incidentally, him* so profoundly does not mean that he creates it in order to express his emotions, nor that he is directing it at ours.

Bryan Magee, we may well think, is incautious; certainly not all Romantic poets would relinquish the conviction that their art had a cognitive function, nor think that lyrical self-expression was its be-all and end-all. Still, we can agree that expression of emotion is *central* to Romantic understanding of art, even as we protest that it is not exhaustive of it, nor definitive of it. As Milosz somewhat ambiguously acknowledges in his reference to Schopenhauer's style—"so logical and precise in its appearance"— Schopenhauer's anti-Romantic allegiance is to be seen most clearly in his deliberate modelling of his German on the English of David Hume.

As for Milosz, he has lately put it on record (*Ironwood,* 1984) that so far from writing being for him a means of self-expression he saw it rather, as T.S. Eliot famously did, as a way of escape from a self deemed to be worthless:

> From the beginning writing was for me a means of redeeming my true or imaginary worthlessness. Perhaps initially it was accompanied by some romantic hope of acquiring an everlasting name. But in reality it was mainly the desire to win merit through edifying literature. Alas, without much success, for I was hampered by the distance between what I felt myself to be and how I would have appeared to my readers.
>
> Of course literature should be edifying. Whoever, because of an exceptionally avid imagination, succumbed to the bad influence of books, cannot think otherwise. The word "edifying" is pronounced sarcastically today and that is proof enough that something is wrong with us. What great works of literature were not edifying? Homer perhaps? Or The Divine Comedy? Or Don Quixote? Or Leaves of Grass?

The inclusion of Whitman in that catalog, along with Homer, Dante, and Cervantes, among authors whose works are undoubtedly "edifying," shows how far Milosz had moved by 1984 from the disparaging estimate of *Song of Myself* which he had voiced twenty years before in *Visions from San Francisco Bay*. And indeed that was inevitable, as it grew upon him that the dithyramb was the appropriate vehicle for what in old age he has come to see as the only truth with which literature can edify: "time: a masque on midsummer night, young girls in bloom, ephemerid generations born and dying in a single hour." There may be—who can doubt that there are?—places in *Leaves of Grass* where Whitman's "I" sinks from the dithyrambic "I" to a shrill and embarrassing lyrical "I"; but the dithyrambic "I" is sufficiently often in control for Milosz nowadays to applaud *Leaves of Grass* as a masterpiece. And indeed, if we take from "A Mirrored Gallery" the phrase "avid, gluttonous," we can see that Milosz has become over the years more and more admiring of, and in tune with, the artists whom he calls "gluttonous"; with Blaise Cendrars, for instance. Now, in 1984, he is prepared to look more favourably even on Henry Miller.

A POSTSCRIPT

What is offered here is a first preliminary "fix" on a writer and thinker who, though he writes in a language and a tradition unfamiliar to English-speakers, must now be accorded by English-speakers something more than bemused deference — and this not merely or chiefly because he has chosen to live among us for the past quarter-century.

Any assessment however must indeed be "preliminary"; that is to say, approximate and tentative. If there had been room for any doubt of this, the doubt would have been dispelled by the appearance, after this essay was completed, of a book by Czeslaw Milosz newly translated: *The Land of Ulro* (in Polish, 1977; in English, 1984). Milosz apologizes for this volume: "I said to myself that a writer can afford to produce in his lifetime one maverick work." But in fact it seems to be the most powerful and compelling of all his prose books in English. It is also the most enlightening: about him, about how his mind works, and about the materials which that mind works on. Because it is indeed "a maverick," however, ascribable to no recognized genre (and without an index even!), it will not enlighten but can only baffle a reader who comes to it without some immersion in Milosz's earlier books, both verse and prose. Thus, having at one point thought of trying to insert in this essay some consideration of *The Land of Ulro*, I came to see that this was impossible without bursting the frame of the earlier discussion, and that that discussion earned its keep precisely as a necessary preparation for engaging with this latest book. Apart from anything else, to have considered this book at the length that it deserves would have meant tilting attention toward Milosz's prose and away from his poems; and this would surely have been a pity. Certainly *The Land of Ulro* prompts some significant changes of emphasis in our sense of Milosz's *oeuvre* as a whole, so far as we have it in English; yet unless I am mistaken, nothing in this latest book positively controverts the conclusions that I have suggested may be drawn out of the earlier work. Rather, certain important matters—for instance, Milosz's sympathy with Manichaean habits of thought, and relatedly the quality of his Roman Catholicism—need no longer be groped after laboriously and hesitantly, since they have now been delineated and defined quite firmly by Milosz himself.

Of the non-Polish authors from the past whom *The Land of Ulro* celebrates as the masters of Milosz's thought if not of his art, few will come as a surprise to those who have read *Emperor of the Earth* in particular. Swedenborg and Dostoievsky, Blake and Simone Weil, especially his elder relative Oscar V. de L. Milosz who wrote in French —Milosz's enthusiastic respect for these names is nothing new. What now emerges more clearly than before, partly because Milosz has dispensed with the protective decorum of the Professor of Literature, is how each of these is linked to the others in his saturnine thinking, and in his perspective on Western culture and society through the last two centuries and more. Other names, notably Goethe and Hölderlin, take on new prominence; and of course the very title gives special prominence to William Blake—an emphasis presumably more interesting and more immediately useful to us anglophones than to the Polish-speakers to whom *The Land of Ulro* originally was addressed.

A particular feature of *The Land of Ulro,* though it figures there (like everything else) only glancingly and incidentally, is Milosz's placing himself in relation to his Polish artistic forebears: Lesmian, Norwid, Wyspianski; Slowacki, Krasinski, others. But what can we do with these names, their work available to us, if at all, only in what are self-evidently clumsy and misleading translations? Very little, I fear. Yet we can do a little better with the Polish poet who by common consent surpasses all these: Mickiewicz. His *Forefathers' Eve,* of enormous import to Milosz as to other Poles, is still concealed from us behind inadequate translations; Mickiewicz's *Pan Tadeusz* we can to some extent grapple with, thanks to a translator of rather long ago, George Rapall Noyes. With nothing but Noyes to go on, no other version to trust or check against, we can take the force of Milosz's contention:

> Despite appearances, despite even the author's own conscious intent, *Pan Tadeusz* is at heart a metaphysical poem, its subject being one

seldom perceived in quotidian reality: *the world of existence as an image of pure Being.* Herein lies the secret of this "last epos in European literature," for *Pan Tadeusz* is not merely a product of a patriarchal social order. It could only have been written by a poet who—in 1849, let us note—once said: "A man's most important books are the calendar and the breviary"; a poet, in other words, in whom the old time-ritualizing ways were vestigially rooted in the agrarian year and in the liturgical year, respectively. Ultimately, only a time measured by sacral standards, and not mechanical clock-time, can sanction a belief in the reality of things.

Mickiewicz is especially important to Milosz because, like Milosz himself, he seems to have conceived of himself, sometimes, as Lithuanian first, only in the second place Polish. The distinction, between Lithuanian-Polish and Polish-Polish, may seem too parochial and too nice for English-speakers to get hold of, or to bother with. But no reader of Milosz's *Native Realm* can think this. Certainly Milosz does not delude himself that in his lifetime his native Lithuania did or could endow him as it endowed Mickiewicz; on the contrary, his drawing attention to the date 1849 should be seen in the context of his argument in *The Land of Ulro* to the effect that already in Mickiewicz's lifetime that endowment—not of talent of course, but of certainty about the sacredness of earth—was extremely rare. On the other hand, it is of the Lithuanian rather than the Polish Mickiewicz that he declares: "If the poetic movement known as Symbolism had not prejudiced our understanding of the term 'symbol,' we might declare the cucumbers and watermelons of the Soplica garden to be eminently worthy of the designation—as things that are both themselves, in the fullness of being, and not themselves." The passage from *Pan Tadeusz* that he has in mind may be this one, which I have ventured to versify from Noyes's sturdy prose:

> Inflamed to re-achieve
> His patrimony, stirred,
> The impressionable Count
> Wandered away. The scene
> Round him, unseeing,
> Changed slowly. Here the green
> Tresses of carrot snared
> Slim beans that stared
> From a thousand eyes; the sage
> And venerable cabbage,

That seemed to meditate
On vegetable fate,
Bared his bald head; the bold
And portly melon rolled
Far from his home, to wait
Upon the flushed estate
Of beetroots; while
Drawn up in file
(Their leaf the snake, their scent
Repels the flies) the hemp
Screened every bed, and a girl
That was Zosia wandered.

It is on the basis of a passage like this (I take it) that Milosz assails what is, he would persuade us, a common formula: Polish equals "rational," Lithuanian equals "mystic." There is, Milosz insists, nothing "mystic" about Mickiewicz's assumption that cucumbers and watermelon take on fullness of being only in a sacral, not a mechanical calendar; and that, if they are symbolic, they are so in a way that does not diminish their earthy fullness and actuality. Milosz himself does not write like this, and he mourns his inability to do so even as he traces the irreversible historical processes which have brought about that incapacity in himself and others.

These concerns may seem remote from what, in earlier pages, I have seemed to be chiefly arguing for: that Milosz, like a few other ambitious poets of his time, refuses to be restricted in his poetry to the lyric *genre* or the lyric mode. But I think I glimpse a connection. For "the sacral," we might say, so long as it is experienced only in discontinuous moments of illumination, is being short-changed—either it informs the whole of our experience, or else it has no firm purchase on any part of it. The lyrical "moment" cedes the initiative to that non-lyrical continuum from which it is, confessedly, an exception. Milosz will not strike that bargain: the imagination cannot be, in his view, restricted to exerting itself in privileged moments; either it governs all our apprehensions, or else it is a marginal and expendable luxury. When more than once he vows himself to practice only writing that shall be "edifying," the word in English makes a witty and far-reaching pun with "edifice"; his writing will edify, in the sense of "educate," "instruct"—but also it will *build,* as the lyric of its nature does not. The lyric acknowledges the pre-eminence of a mode of experience, prudential or mundane or scientific, from which it is the privileged exception. As Milosz represents them in *The Land of Ulro,* Goethe and Blake and Hölderlin refused to make that acknowledgment; and so does Milosz refuse it.

APPENDIX
Milosz's War-Time Poems

Reviewing Milosz's *Selected Poems,* the poet-translator Clayton Eshleman (*Los Angeles Times,* 5 July 1981) found himself affronted by lines from a poem called "Dedication," carefully dated "1945":

> What is poetry which does not save
> Nations or people?
> A connivance with official lies.
> A song of drunkards whose throats will be cut in a moment.
> Readings for sophomore girls.
> That I wanted good poetry without knowing it,
> That I discovered, late, its salutary aim,
> In this and only this I find salvation.

Eshleman protested he could not accept that if poetry does not meet the, for him, exorbitant requirements of the first two lines, it is doomed to nothing better than the contemptible or at best marginal status that the next three lines assign to it. He admitted that this response was conditioned by his being an American, and that he might have felt differently if he had been a Pole who spent the 1940s in Warsaw. Even so, he decided, "I find myself saying that no serious poetry 'saves nations or people.'"

We must be thankful that Eshleman is so forthright, for he is here grappling with one of the most troublesome issues of post-1945 poetry, troublesome at least for those peoples, like the British or the American, whose experiences of World War II were in general less harrowing than that of other peoples like the Poles or the European Jews. The disparity between the one sort of historical experience and the other has at times been exploited to furnish moral blackmail, by which a single word like "Ravensbruck" or "Auschwitz" is invoked so as to shame into silence all English-language poets, indeed (in its most extravagant form) so as to silence all poets whatever, in whatever language. This is obviously intolerable. And indeed it is something worse than that; for in effect, in such an argument, the sufferings of thousands dead are being used so as to claim a moral superiority for one party over another among the living. It is important to recognize that a poem like "Dedication" is not advancing such a disgraceful argument, nor exerting any such blackmail. If it were, then the protest implicit in Eshleman's remarks would be abundantly justifiable; although in Warsaw in 1945 the choice between a responsible and a humanly irresponsible poetry may indeed have presented itself as starkly as it did for Milosz at that time in that place, it could not so present itself to anyone in Los Angeles (or London) in 1981. Moreover poets in those cities (there have been some) who would pretend that the issue before them *is* so stark can do so only by slighting the American or British experience that they know at first hand, in favor of a Polish or a Jewish experience that they can know only vicariously. It cannot be the case that, to write a responsible poetry now and ensure it in the future, American and British poets in the 1980s must imagine themselves back into Warsaw in the 1940s.

Yet if this is not what Milosz is saying in a poem like "Dedication," what *is* he saying—to us who now read him in English? Just there, however, is the misunderstanding. For in "Dedication" as in most of the other poems of the 1940s which are grouped with it in the third section of *Selected Poems* (1980), Milosz is not addressing us or concerning himself with our situation. As English-speakers we merely overhear an address made in Polish by one Pole to other Poles, living or dead. It may seem that this is true of all Milosz's poems, or of all the poems earlier than "The Spirit of the Laws" (1947), where he seems to be already working with scenes from Washington, D.C. But in fact this is not true of some even earlier poems. For what we find ourselves saying, so as to assure Clayton Eshleman that he should not have felt put on the defensive, is that the "I" which speaks "Dedication" is the lyrical "I," whose reflections are to be taken as true only to a specific occasion, a special place at a special time. It is for that reason, and not at all so as to bully us into feeling unfounded shame or guilt, that "Dedication" and "Song of a Citizen," "A Poor Christian Looks at the Ghetto" and "Café," "The Poor Poet" and "Outskirts," "A Song on the End of the World" and "Mid-Twentieth-Century Portrait" are all scrupulously dated in the 1940s and declared as from either Warsaw or Cracow. Accordingly, if there is shame and guilt in these poems, as there is, it is a shame and guilt peculiar to Milosz himself. These are indeed among the most personal poems he has ever written, and accordingly, once we learn that we are not being "got at" or "put down," we shall find it easier to appreciate these poems than others by Milosz. For "personal lyric" is the sort of poetry that most of us look for, to the point where some of us forget that other sorts of poems are possible, and are still being written.

Milosz, we have seen, is ambitious of performing in other *genres* than this. At least we have found reasons for thinking so. Accordingly, the question arises: did he not find some one of those other *genres* appropriate for embodying his experience of Warsaw under the Nazi occupation?

He did: and not retrospectively either, but from out of the midst of the experience, or from the worst of it. And the form he found to fit his purpose was, of all the traditional *genres,* that one which at first blush seems least likely; it was the idyll. Of this idyll, a poem or sequence of poems in twenty parts, the *Selected Poems* gives us just one such part: the poem, significantly without date or by-line, called "Recovery." The translation reads poorly as a poem in English, and has lately been much improved on, by Robert Pinsky and Robert Hass. For Pinsky and Hass, with a disinterestedness that does them much credit and earns our rather fervent gratitude, have lately made available this work, "The World: A Naïve Poem," in *The Separate Notebooks* (1984). In *Selected Poems* "Recovery" is noted as "from 'The World,' poem in a primer's rhyme." This formulation is doubtless Milosz's own, for this is how he speaks of this work elsewhere, for instance in his *History of Polish Literature* (1969, p. 459): "*The World,* a long poem of Milosz's, written in 1943, is one of the most serene in modern Polish literature. Its 'primerlike' quatrains describe the beauty of the simplest things and exemplify the effort to resist the temptation of utter despair." Unfortunately "primer's rhyme" and "primerlike" and even the word "primer" itself are not so self-explanatory to an English-speaker as Milosz supposes. To those Anglophone readers who can attach any meaning at all to these expressions, they probably signify: "as simple as a child's ABC." And Milosz means that, but also means rather more — as Robert Hass,

for one, has understood. For in his valuable brief note on how he
and Pinsky approached the translating of this work, Hass notes that,
when Milosz wrote the poem, he was teaching himself English by
reading William Blake. And Hass remarks: "It seems clear that Blake's
'Songs of Innocence' provided Milosz with a means." Why then did
Pinsky and Hass, when they looked for an English idiom to trans-
late the poem into, not go to "Songs of Innocence"? If we remind
ourselves what "Songs of Innocence" are like, we can find the answer
for ourselves. Hass's explanation is satisfying and highly intelligent,
but elliptical, and therefore to some will seem cryptic:

> Would Blake's "Songs of Innocence" be a model? Not quite. More like
> a child's primer. How about Stevenson's *A Child's Garden of Verses*?
> Closer, but not quite. Nursery rhymes? Well, no, more tranquil than
> nursery rhymes. Then maybe, "How doth the Busy Bumblebee"? Yes,
> but the tone is fresh, it is not an adult talking down to children.
> (*PN Review*, 27)

I shall return to this.

Milosz writes briefly of Blake — alas in what in translation is very
clumsy English — in an essay in *Visions from San Francisco Bay* (pp.
177–78), where he makes the certainly important and perennially
necessary point that, whereas Blake is certainly anti-rationalist, he
is not therefore opposed to Reason, still less to Intellect. This should
be emphasized because Milosz, despite strenuously explicit protesta-
tions on his part, can still be treated as an anti-intellectual himself
(e.g. by a reviewer in *The Nation*, 13 June 1981). And certainly one
good way into Milosz would be by following the William Blake who
exclaimed, "Is the Holy Ghost any other than an intellectual foun-
tain?" However, a more immediately available gloss on "The World"
(which is hard to gloss just because it is so limpid) is in certain passages of Milosz's lecture when accepting the Nobel prize. In particular Milosz speaks there of a seventeenth-century Latin poem by
Casimire Sarbiewski in which the poet "describes his voyage — on the
back of Pegasus — from Vilno to Antwerp, where he is going to visit
his poet friends . . . he beholds under him rivers, lakes, forests; that
is, a map, both distant and yet concrete." There is an obvious relation between this and the tenth poem in "The World," which is called,
in Robert Pinsky's beautiful translation, "Father Explains":

There, where a long streak of sun touches the plain
And shadows move as if they really did run,
Stands Warsaw, open on all sides to the world:
A famous town, though not so very old.

Farther, where the slant threads of rain fall
Onto those hills covered with acacia trees,
Is Prague, with its castle built on the highest hill,
As the custom of ancient city-builders was.

The white foam that rises to divide the land
We call the Alps, and there where you can see
Only darkness is fir-tree forest. And beyond,
Like a deep blue dish, lies all of Italy.

Among its many beautiful towns, you can tell Rome,
Christendom's capital city, by that sphere-shaped arch,
Repeated along the roofline; it is the dome
Of the basilica, Saint Peter's church.

And there, North, where a plain rises and slopes
Through blue mists, past where the sea's bay reaches,
Paris curves upward like a stone tower's steps,
Above the river where it keeps its flock of bridges.

And along with Paris there are other towns,
Glass-adorned and iron-bound; but to say
More about them would be too much for this once:
The rest I will tell you some other day.

What is the height from which one can see Warsaw, Rome, and Paris at once, and yet see in Rome the dome of St. Peter's? There can be no such vantage-point, we say. And yet we are wrong, for the vantage-point is in the awareness of the father as he pores with his children over a map of Europe, explaining what they see and elaborating on it so as to begin conveying his vantage-point over to them. What for Sarbiewski could be managed only by Pegasus, the poetic imagination, is in this poem managed by father-as-teacher. And the seeming double-focus—which is really a single focus, in which we see Rome in relation to Prague and yet can pick out St. Peter's, the map "both distant and yet concrete"—is elsewhere in the Nobel lecture declared to be the focus that the poet must aim at and sometimes attain, solving then, for a moment or an hour, the problem of universals, by reconciling the general with the particular.

It should now be clear why "Songs of Innocence" wouldn't serve

Pinsky and Hass as a model. What Milosz writes are songs of Innocence-seeking-Experience. His idyll is an idyll of education; better, of apprenticeship; better still, of initiation. Accordingly Hass and Pinsky showed great insight when, looking for a serviceable idiom, they back-tracked from Blake to those predecessors we know he was aware of, writers of poems for children who were however didactic as Blake did not want to be; in particular to one such predecessor, Isaac Watts, author of "How doth the little busy bee." But there the problem was, as Hass duly remarks, that Watts writes always as the adult, the teacher, addressing the child, the pupil; whereas what gives to "The World" its idyllic character is that Milosz's poems are uttered always by the child as *eager* apprentice, *willing* pupil. (It is worth remarking that, after Watts but before Blake, precisely this idyllic stance is to be found in a poem like "Moderation" from Christopher Smart's *Hymns for the Amusement of Children* — a model that might have served Pinsky and Hass, if they had thought of it.)

"The World," then, is an idyll of education, as seen from the standpoint of the taught rather than the teacher; and *that* is what Milosz meant, when he spoke of "a primer." In the first poem we have the boy and the girl coming home from school. But in fact they are going home *to* school; for the assumption throughout the poem is that the education that matters is pursued inside the household, with the mother and father as the teachers. At the end of the poem the children come in sight of the father working in his garden:

> From his tilled patch, he can see the whole region.

Literally of course he cannot; but really and essentially he can. By virtue of having just and informed knowledge of how his own activities lock in with those of his neighbors (and it is not for nothing, surely, that we see him engaged in husbandry), the man "sees," has an accurate and inclusive perception of, all his neighborhood. It is, on a reduced scale, just what Sarbiewski saw from the back of Pegasus; at once generalized and particular. The second poem is called "The Gate" and through that, naturally enough, the children pass so as to reach, in the third poem, "The Porch." Here already their education begins — at a stage when not yet words but only pictures can acquaint them with violence, and the organized violence that is war:

> A pink tongue between lips helps along the careful
> Great shapes of warships, one of which goes under.

(And compliments, incidentally, on the nicely judged step of epithets across that line-ending. Very workmanlike, Mr. Pinsky!) The next poem, "The Dining Room" introduces the mother. Great pains have been taken, throughout the sequence, to balance the mother's role against the father's; yet the mother's role is more elusive, and harder to do justice to. Here, as she serves a meal to the chiming of clocks, she is seen to provide, along with security and sustenance, an example of timeliness, of regularity, timely ordering. She is the principal figure in the next poem also, where her shadow as she descends the stairs meshes with the shadow of a boar's head, mounted on the staircase wall:

> And so she struggles, alone, with the menacing beast.

Literally, she does not; but truly, she does. And the implications of the trope surely need not be teased out. In the next poem, "Pictures," the children are still at a pre-verbal stage of their education; and already at that stage they can be introduced to classical antiquity as, turning from a picture of the death of Hector, they move from ancient Greece to ancient Rome, with a picture of Cincinnatus:

> Nearby, his oxen grunting at their steady labour,
> A naked ploughman works a hillside farm.

At this point, with two quatrains ("Father in the Library") conveying the children's wonderment at the magical phenomenon of reading, a skill they are now to learn, we move into what may be called relatively *formal* education:

> Only one whom God has taught magic
> Could know the marvels his book reveals.

("Marvels," wonderment—learning begins in *wonder*; it is Aristotelean doctrine.) And from this point forward one can, not altogether fancifully, plot the curriculum. It begins with "Father's Invocation" which, as handsomely translated by Robert Hass, inaugurates the whole enterprise by invoking the splendor of the humanist tradition:

> Men are small, their works are great.

The first lesson thereafter is in geography, and "Father Explains" is the second half of it. The second lesson is, we may say, in astronomy, though the poem in question, "Parable of the Poppy-seed," has also profound ethical implications, as we shall see:

> The earth is a seed, and nothing more.
> And that seed's a planet, and that seed's a star.
> And even if there were a hundred thousand
> Each seed would contain a house and a garden.

The poem may be imagined as spoken by either the Father or the Mother, though it is better and more affecting to think of all these poems as spoken by one or other of the children wonderingly repeating what they suppose one of the parents has told them. The instruction now becomes religious, inaugurated by the mother inculcating by example the virtues of trustfulness and courage:

> Nothing of what she thinks
> Is she afraid to say to herself outright.
> Or to the children. The sun in the leaves
> Casts shadows on their faces, and speckled light.

And the religious instruction proceeds by way of three poems celebrating in order the three Pauline virtues: Faith, Hope, Charity. The next lesson after that, in the poems "An Outing to the Forest" and "The Bird Kingdom," may be called a lesson in natural history— important if we remember from *Native Realm* and also *Bells in Winter* what a prominent place Milosz assigns to that in his own education as he remembers it. By this stage the children's education is already far advanced and becoming exacting, as we see when the title "Fear" announces the lesson they must learn next. The fear in question is occasioned by the seeming withdrawal of the father-figure, who may be God the Father; and "Recovery," the piece that was put in *Selected Poems,* recounts the escape from fear when the father-figure's presence is seen to have been constant, never withdrawn despite appearances to the contrary. (Milosz, we remember, has declared that the poems of this sequence "exemplify the effort to resist the temptation of utter despair"—a temptation that, in Warsaw in 1943, must have been pressing.) The last piece, "The Sun," is a lesson in aesthetics:

And anyone who wants to take his brush and try
To paint the Earth must not look straight up at the Sun
Or he will lose the memory of all he's ever seen,
With only a burning tear to fill his eye.

Let him kneel down and press his cheek in grass and then
Look till he sees the beam the Earth reflects back upwards.
There he will find all of our lost, forgotten treasures;
Stars and Roses, the setting and the rising Sun.

Art, that is, must proceed by indirections and can express the universal only by way of the particular and contingent.

The moral philosopher Alasdair MacIntyre has asserted (*After Virtue: A Study in Moral Theory* (London, 1981, p. 240):

> To cut oneself off from shared activity in which one has initially to learn obediently as an apprentice learns, to isolate oneself from the communities which find their point and purpose in such activities, will be to debar oneself from finding any good outside of oneself. It will be to condemn oneself to that moral solipsism which constitutes Nietzschean greatness.

This is part of MacIntyre's explanation of the ethical system of Aristotle, which is rather plainly the only such system that MacIntyre finds well grounded—a system in which there is no room for the concept of "human rights," or for any notion that we have rights by virtue of being human rather than being part of some one humanly constituted community. Since the Enlightenment, anti-Aristotelean theories of the virtues have attempted—unsuccessfully, in MacIntyre's view—to ground the learning of the virtues elsewhere than in such communities and such apprenticeships. All Milosz's testimonies, early and late, suggest that he would be, with MacIntyre, on the Aristotelean side in this debate; and indeed I take the burden or (better) the tacit assumption of "The World: A Naïve Poem" to be just the sentences that I have quoted from MacIntyre. It is notable however that for Aristotle, as MacIntyre understands and expounds him, the community in question, which can give grounds for the virtues and instruction in them, is nothing less extensive than the *polis,* the community of free citizens in a city-state, though I take it that subordinate communities, as of fellow-artificers in a vocational guild, are also in the Aristotelean scheme allowed for and approved. Thus even the ethical systems which the Aristotelean system is held to have superseded, those of the Heroic Age, take for granted, as the ambiance in which virtues and obligations can be meaningful, a kinship system more elaborate than what anthropologists have taught us to describe, apologetically, as "the nuclear family." In Milosz's idyll, however, the nuclear family (father, mother, and children) is assumed and by implication declared to be a thoroughly adequate community for the purposes of apprenticeship and initiation. There is nowhere an acknowledgment that of such Aristotelean communities the nuclear family is a specially late-come, narrow, and precarious instance. It may well be thought that this is what makes "The World," though formally and generically so surprising, a thoroughly modern work, and certainly not restricted in significance by the Lithuanian/Polish matrix that it emerges from. For the nuclear family is indeed in the modern world the only nub or residue of the *polis* that effectively survives; and it does not survive universally nor easily, as we all know. The nuclear family is, for good or ill, as much of community as widely persists among us; and if the Aristotelean virtues are to be preserved by us and handed down to the next generation, this confined and endangered unit of community is the only context in which that cultural duty can be discharged.

In "The World," the poem called "Faith" is concerned not in the first place with faith in God, but with faith in the objective reality of a world to be known by the human mind but not constituted by that mind, still less amenable to manipulations and transformations effected by that human consciousness which observes it or contemplates it. So too with "Hope":

> *Hope* means that someone believes the earth
> Is not a dream, that it is living flesh;
> That sight, touch, hearing tell the truth;
> And that all the things we have known here
> Are like a garden, looked at from the gate. . . .
>
> . . . Some people think our eyes deceive us; they say
> That there is nothing but a pretty seeming:
> And just these are the ones who don't have hope.
> They think that when a person turns away
> The whole world vanishes behind his back
> As if a clever thief had snatched it up.

The poet who could say this, in the deliberately naïve accents of childhood, was consistent with the one who, in the Nobel lecture nearly forty years later, would protest: "whoever considers writing poetry as 'to see and describe' should be aware that he engages in a quarrel with modernity, fascinated as it is with innumerable theories of a specific poetic language." Elsewhere in the Nobel lecture, on an occasion when it might have been thought that polemic was out of place, Milosz said: "There is, it seems, a hidden link between theories of literature as *écriture,* of speech feeding on itself, and the growth of the totalitarian state." And in the last sentences of his lecture Milosz rubs again at what is for him, it seems, a persistent sore: "Memory thus is our force; it protects us against a speech entwining upon itself like the ivy when it does not find a support on a tree or a wall." Milosz is surely mistaken; his quarrel is not with "modernity" but with *modernism,* or at all events with that strain of modernism which, coming out of *symbolisme* and taking off from a false understanding of the Berkeleyan *esse est percipi* ("when a person turns away / The whole world vanishes behind his back"), has declared the artist to be under no obligation to anything but the structure of his own sensibility. For Milosz the world is real, and it is other; it is not to be shrunken inside the confines of the language which, not always nor everywhere fraudulently, claims to name that world and to articulate it.

Among the constituents of a world thus a *datum,* a "given," there figures the household, the nuclear family:

> The earth is a seed, and nothing more,
> And that seed's a planet, and that seed's a star.
> And even if there were a hundred thousand
> Each seed would contain a house and a garden.
>
> All in a poppyhead. They grow taller than hay.
> The children run through, and the poppy plants sway.
> And, in the evening, when the moon is aloft,
> You hear the dogs barking, first loudly then soft.

Mother, and father, and their children . . . they constitute "a house and a garden"; so many households, each guarded by its watch dog. And the communal unit which the household constitutes is declared to be, not the transient phenomenon of one sort of social organization among others through the ages, but on the contrary part of the nature of things, as much so as the structure of a poppy-head, or the planetary system.

Hass and Pinsky were told by their Polish-speaking informants, Lillian Vallee and Renata Gorczynski, that if only they had had command of Polish they would have found the idiom of "The World" near to that of Mickiewicz in some parts of *Pan Tadeusz*. As Hass points out humorously, it was impossible for him and Pinsky to profit by this information. Yet it has this importance: that, whereas those who heard the poem read at clandestine gatherings under the Occupation were understandably baffled and disconcerted by its apparent remoteness from historical circumstances, yet Milosz was not attempting the unprecedented. That, it seems, was never his habit. On the contrary, as he remarks of himself (*Postwar Polish Poetry,* Harmondsworth, 1970, p. 57), "The term 'classicism' applied to his poetry probably means that his experimentation is mitigated by an attachment to old Polish verse." And it is true that "the idyll" was a *genre* practiced in Poland long before Mickiewicz. As for those parts of *Pan Tadeusz* which seem to belong in this tradition, it is worth remarking that they seem to be related to "The World" not just stylistically but in substance also. For one facet of the multifaceted *Pan Tadeusz* is concerned precisely with the apprenticeship or initiation of the young and callow Tadeusz in or into an ancestral household conceived of as a fount of moral learning.

SELECTED BOOKS

BY CZESLAW MILOSZ

The books by Czeslaw Milosz cited in this study,
in English or translated into English, are:

The Captive Mind (New York, 1953)
The Seizure of Power (New York, 1955)
Native Realm: A Search for Self-Definition (New York, 1968)
The History of Polish Literature (New York, 1969)
Emperor of the Earth: Modes of Eccentric Vision (Berkeley, 1977)
Bells in Winter (New York and Manchester, 1980)
Selected Poems (1980) (New York and Toronto, 1980)
Visions from San Francisco Bay (New York, 1982)
The Witness of Poetry (Cambridge, Mass., and London, 1983)
The Land of Ulro (New York, 1984)
The Separate Notebooks (New York, 1984)

EDITED AND/OR TRANSLATED BY CZESLAW MILOSZ ARE:

Selected Poems by Zbigniew Herbert [with Peter Dale Scott] (Harmonds-
worth, 1968)
Postwar Polish Poetry: An Anthology (Harmondsworth, 1970; Berkeley, 1983)
Mediterranean Poems by Aleksander Wat (Ann Arbor, 1977)
The Noble Traveller; selected works by Oscar Milosz (New York, 1983)

OTHER WORKS

Books by other authors cited in the text are identified
where they occur, except for the following:

J.B. Yeats, *Letters to his son W.B. Yeats and others 1869–1922,* edited with
a memoir by Joseph Hone (London, 1954)
Boris Pasternak, *Poems,* translated by Eugene M. Kayden (Ann Arbor, 1959)
Donald Davie, *The Forests of Lithuania* (Hessle, 1959)

INDEX

The Hodges Lectures

THE BETTER ENGLISH FUND was established in 1947 by John C. Hodges, Professor of English, The University of Tennessee, 1921–1962, and head of the English Department, 1941–1962, on the returns from the *Harbrace College Handbook,* of which he was the author. Over the years, it has been used to support the improvement of teaching and research in the English Department. The Hodges Lectures are intended to commemorate this wise and generous bequest.

VOLUMES PUBLISHED

Theodore Roosevelt Among the Humorists: W.D. Howells, Mark Twain, and Mr. Dooley, by William M. Gibson.
Arts on the Level: The Fall of the Elite Object, by Murray Krieger.
Books and Painting: Shakespeare, Milton, and the Bible: Literary Texts and the Emergence of English Painting, by Ronald Paulson.
Wallace Stevens: Words Chosen Out of Desire, by Helen Vendler.
Beowulf and the Appositive Style, by Fred C. Robinson
The Romantic Body: Love and Sexuality in Keats, Wordsworth, and Blake, by Jean H. Hagstrum.

THE HODGES LECTURES book series is set in ten-point Sabon type with two-point spacing between the lines. Sabon is also used for display. The series format was designed by Jim Billingsley. This title in the series was composed by Metricomp of Grundy Center, Iowa, printed by Thomson-Shore, Inc., Dexter, Michigan, and bound by John H. Dekker & Sons, Grand Rapids, Michigan. The paper on which the book is printed bears the watermark of S.D. Warren and is designed for an effective life of at least 300 years.

THE UNIVERSITY OF TENNESSEE PRESS : KNOXVILLE